PROBLEMS IN EDUCATION

JONAS F. SOLTIS
Professor of Philosophy and Education
Teachers College, Columbia University

and

JONATHAN C. MESSERLI
Dean, School of Education
Hofstra University

Series Editors

In every age educators not only face new problems unique to their times, but also redefine many old problems in light of present conditions. This series is intended to provide anthologies containing comprehensive sets of readings which directly address themselves to some single major contemporary issue in educational scholarship, theory, or practice. The purpose of the series is not merely to inform students and educators about important contemporary problems, but to inform their thinking about these problems so that they may deal with them more wisely and effectively.

Moral Education

BARRY I. CHAZAN

and

JONAS F. SOLTIS

Editors

TEACHERS COLLEGE PRESS
Teachers College, Columbia University
NEW YORK & LONDON

Second Printing, 1974

© 1973 by Teachers College, Columbia University
Library of Congress Catalog Card Number: 72-89127

Manufactured in the United States of America

TO MY PARENTS

Barry Chazan

Preface

In those critical times when a society finds its basic values questioned and even rejected by some groups, more often than not institutions of education are blamed for the failure to instill proper values in the young, and they respond with serious efforts to provide some effective form of moral education. The task of transmitting values to our children to insure a morally sound society while at the same time providing freedom of choice in moral matters has been a focal concern of philosophers and educators throughout the centuries, and it is no less a problem today. Thus, in response to various contemporary "value crises," many concerned educators are turning to deeper study of the problems and issues of moral education.

This volume, then, should be a welcome addition to the Problems in Education series, in that it provides an ingredient essential to the thoughtful design and implementation of effective programs in moral education—a serious consideration of the nature of morality and the key features of the moral situation viewed from the perspective of the prospective moral educator. Too often, well-intended programs in moral education are theoretically unsophisticated and theoretical discussions of sophisticated moral philosophers are too technical to be practically relevant. Bridging the gap between theory and practice is never an easy task. What this volume offers is the means to do so for those who would dare to try.

JONAS F. SOLTIS

Contents

Moral Education

General Introduction

The most striking characteristic of the contemporary state of moral education is the inconsistency between what is said and what is done. Numerous formal statements of educational aims affirm the centrality of the goal of developing morally responsible citizens through public schooling; yet few schools actually deal with moral education in a serious and systematic fashion. Civil, political, and educational leaders frequently cite education's crucial role in the transmission of those "moral and spiritual values" necessary for life in today's complex world; yet few educational systems make formal provision for such value education. The teacher is often proclaimed to be the central force in the formation of moral character in the young; yet few teachers have been provided with training designed to enhance their effectiveness as moral educators. In short, there exists an uncomfortable dichotomy between the official language and the actual practice of contemporary moral education.

If we do not deny the sincerity of those who speak the "official language," then it should be clear that a fundamental problem in contemporary moral education is the inability of those with good intentions to effectively translate genuine moral concerns into significant educational programs. We believe that one of the primary reasons for this inability has been the lack of communication between the moral philosopher and the moral educator. The philosopher has rarely attempted

1

2 MORAL EDUCATION

to speak directly to the central issues of moral education; and the educator has infrequently availed himself of the rich literature in moral philosophy which contains ideas fundamental to an understanding of the moral situation. The result has been that most practical attempts at moral education have been theoretically superficial while the technical discussions in moral philosophy have been for practical purposes irrelevant.

This volume is intended to help bridge the gap between the moral philosopher and the moral educator by providing selected discussions of significant themes in moral philosophy in a way that may enable those concerned about moral education to more fully understand the complex nature of their task. Readings have been drawn primarily from the most readable contemporary sources in moral philosophy and philosophy of education. They have been arranged to lead initially from a broad consideration of the question "How do we know what is moral?" to focused discussions of problems more directly related to the teaching of moral values. There are selections which deal with the forms of moral justification, the nature of moral principles, the logic of moral thinking, and the relationship between moral knowledge and moral action. Before turning directly to the selections, however, it may be useful to provide some background ideas essential to seeing the selections in perspective as they relate to the key issues and questions of moral education.

MORALIZING AND MORAL PHILOSOPHY

There frequently is confusion in ordinary language between two forms of thinking and talking about moral issues—moralizing and moral philosophy.[1]

"Moralizing" refers to the offering of judgements about *specific* principles, values, and behaviors deemed as "immoral" or "moral" in a particular society. Thus moralizing is a dominant form of criticism of a society and is used as a means to urge a change in the moral point of

[1]See the following for discussions of this confusion: W. Frankena, *Ethics*, pp. 1-10 (reprinted here in Ch. I); S. Toulmin, *An Examination of the Place of Reason in Ethics* (Cambridge: Cambridge University Press, 1960), pp. 170-181.

view of members of the society. The objective of such moralizing activity, then, is both evaluative and educational, and it involves concern with the following sorts of problems: the erosion of moral values among the young (i.e., the fact that the young question and may even discard values regarded as "moral" by their elders); the "valuelessness" of modern culture (meaning that modern culture is not consistent with traditionally held values); the moral propriety of official government acts (critiques of war, poverty, inequity in the law, and so forth); the moral neutrality of university academicians (meaning that professors do not tell students how to act "properly"). The concern of the moralist in such cases is to examine the consistency of actual behavior with postulated norms as well as to question the validity of accepted or proposed norms. The language of moralizing is usually emotive and passionate because of the evaluative and educational tasks of the moralist. The moralizing function is not unique to any one category of individuals, and in practice it has been assumed by such disparate figures as—to mention only a few—prophets, clergymen, playwrights, poets, painters, novelists, politicians, professors, folk singers, and newscasters. However, it certainly is not the case that the moral philosopher is automatically or necessarily ever acting as a moralist (or vice versa), as we shall see below.

Moralizing is an indispensable aspect of social life, for it is a means of evaluating adherence to accepted principles, of preventing too dangerous deviation from accepted principles, and of enabling periodic modifications of accepted principles. Thus, proclamations about "the contemporary malaise" of our society[2] or descriptions of our age as "a world adrift"[3] are of value if they help us to re-examine and re-evaluate our most basic values and behaviors. (Of course it is another matter whether the contemporary malaise is any worse than the traditional or future malaise, or whether our world is any more adrift now than in any other age.) Indeed, a tradition of thoughtful moralizing is the crucial mechanism a creative society utilizes for the prevention of either moral anarchy or moral totalitarianism.

[2]R. S. Peters, *Authority, Responsibility, and Education* (New York: Atherton Press, 1966), Ch. 4.

[3]Sir Richard Livingston, *Education for a World Adrift* (New York: Macmillan, 1944).

A second form of talking and thinking about moral issues is "moral philosophizing." Unlike moralizing, moral philosophy is concerned not with the observation, evaluation, and critique of *particular* societal values and behaviors, but with the more *general* and *rational* study of the nature of moral concepts, problems, and issues.

Moral philosophy may be divided into analytic and synthetic moral philosophy. *Analytic* moral philosophy is concerned with the following activities:

1. The analysis of concepts used in the moral sphere and in moral discussions; e.g., good, right, wrong, moral, value, indoctrination, evil.

2. The analysis of central problems of the moral sphere; e.g., the role of reason in ethics, autonomy versus habit in morality, the nature of the justification of moral decisions.

3. The delineation of the nature of the moral sphere itself (as distinguished, for example, from the religious, the political, or the aesthetic).

Synthetic moral philosophy encompasses these same activities of analytic moral philosophy while also involving a fourth function:

4. The development of systematic answers to the problems and issues raised in analytic moral philosophy. The synthetic moral philosopher is concerned not only with indicating how the term "good" has been used, or with what are the different approaches to moral justification, but also with actually indicating what the Good *is* or *should be* and how moral decisions *should be* justified.

Synthetic moral philosophy, then, is in one sense similar to moralizing; both have a clearly normative function. However, these two activities differ in the following significant ways:

1. Synthetic moral philosophy is rooted in the intensive rational analysis of meanings, rather than in the critique of observed social norms or behaviors.

2. Synthetic moral philosophy is not, as is moralizing, exclusively motivated by or aimed at *behavior;* it is concerned rather with the nature of morality and of the Good Life.

3. Moralizing is local to a particular situation and a particular society; synthetic moral philosophy aims at a level of generality which transcends purely local boundaries.

Thus, while the moralist and the moral philosopher both deal with the moral sphere and the moral life, they do so from different perspectives and with different objectives.

Ideally, there should be a dynamic relationship and interaction between moralizing and moral philosophy. The moral philosopher is important to the moralist in that he clarifies basic assumptions, terminology, and conceptual apparatus and even provides justifiable moral systems. The moralist is important to the moral philosopher in that he guarantees that the latter does not lose sight of the ultimately practical and behavioral base of the real-life moral sphere. It also should be apparent that *both* moralizing and moral philosophy can provide important contributions to the development of programs in moral education. As noted, however, the predominant theoretical influence upon moral education has been moralizing, with moral philosophy having had a negligible impact. The literature of moral education programs reflects the moralist's passionate demands for strengthening the moral character of the young and for confronting the moral crises that face a contemporary society.[4] However, while the institution of programs in moral education has been motivated by genuine concern for the Good Life, most if not all have been devoid of the critical thinking and clarification associated with moral philosophy. The result is that while moral education has been rich in moral fervor, it has been lacking in conceptual depth. The moral life is certainly a life of fervor, but it is also a life of careful thought and deliberative choice. It is precisely this balance which is absent in much that passes for contemporary moral education.

THE CONTRIBUTION OF MORAL PHILOSOPHY TO MORAL EDUCATION

We have claimed that moral philosophy has a significant contribution to make to moral education. In some instances this contribution is reflected in the application of philosophic method to the issues of moral education. In addition, moral philosophy has an important contribution to make through a corpus of discussions and conclusions about the nature of the moral sphere.

[4]See, for example, the description of the "Kentucky Movement" program of moral education in: E. F. Hartford, *Moral Values in Public Education* (New York: Harper and Brothers, 1959); and W. Bower, *Moral and Spiritual Values in Education* (Lexington: University of Kentucky Press, 1952).

Common Assumptions

In this section we shall discuss three themes of moral philosophy, to be called "common assumptions of moral philosophy," which may be regarded as essential theoretical components of any discussion of moral philosophy and of the theory and practice of moral education. The discussion will reflect our view of the dominant accepted axioms of tradidional and contemporary moral philosophy which we believe are indispensable and basic to any attempt to develop an effective theory and practice of moral education.

1. The first common assumption of contemporary moral philosophy is the position that the terms "moral" and "morality" do not simply refer *either* to behavior *or* to attitudes, but rather refer to a complex of components which encompass at least <u>both</u> of these elements. That is, according to this assumption, the notions of "moral" and "morality" include as minimal and indispensable components both *attitudes* and *behaviors*. This means that the moral sphere is related to the performance of certain behaviors (e.g., *care* for the sick, *charity* for the poor, *aid* to the elderly), but that it is not *simply* behavioral. In addition, the moral sphere also involves certain types of motivations, dispositions, and intentions which are indispensable preconditions for moral behavior (e.g., *love* of mankind, *honor* of elders, *respect* for human life).

This first claim, then, constitutes a rejection of two polarized notions of the moral sphere and morality: as exclusively a question of proper behaviors, with intention being irrelevant; or as exclusively a question of intentions, with the consequent behaviors being secondary or irrelevant. Instead, our view of moral philosophy emphasizes the centrality of both elements for an accurate definition of "moral" and "morality."

Indeed, the very way people talk about morality verifies this point. There is a reluctance to call the person who performs all the "proper" and acceptable behaviors of a certain society "moral" without any reference to his motives and *just because* he performs those behaviors. Even in cases where we do call such a person "moral," there is a need to add a qualifying or limiting phrase of the following sort. "He is 'moral' *in the sense* that he performs proper behaviors, but his 'morality' is other-directed or *external*." That is, our very usage of the word "moral" prohibits an exclusively behavioristic sense of the term and forces a consideration of the reasons behind overt moral actions. Similarly, we would certainly be reluctant to call someone "moral" only because of his good intentions. We do speak of people "who mean well" or "who have good intentions," but this is not meant to equate them simplistically with "being moral" without reference to their explicit behavior. If we do describe such a person as "moral," we still feel the need to qualify or explain further: "He meant well, *but . . .,*" or "He had good intentions, *but* they didn't lead to moral actions." Thus, according to our first common assumption, moral man, the moral sphere, and morality, all, at least minimally, refer to certain sorts of *actions* related to certain sorts of *attitudes, intentions,* and *dispositions.* This assumption constitutes a rejection of any simplified notion of the moral-life-sphere as either exclusively behavioral or singularly contemplative.

Acceptance of this first common assumption wreaks havoc with many of the existent programs of moral education which have been rooted in one or the other of the simplistic positions just cited. This common assumption directly contradicts the underlying assumptions *both* of behavior-focused programs exclusively concerned with the development and replication of moral behaviors (religious education is often taken as the paradigm of such an approach) *and* of attitude-focused programs that emphasize intention without its behavioral correlative (e.g., programs aimed solely at development of the affective domain). The implication of this first common assumption is that moral education is a broadly based and comprehensive activity concerned with the devlopment of intentions which are related to and manifest themselves in specific behaviors.

2. A second common assumption of contemporary moral philosophy is that the concept "morality" does not simply or solely refer to mores or behaviors deemed acceptable in a certain society, but also refers to the act of personal confrontation with and choice between alternative principles and behaviors on the basis of criteria that transcend the value system of any particular society.

The importance of this common assumption lies in its rejection of a one-sided notion of morality as concerned only with compulsory and fixed social behaviors. It is surely true that the moral sphere does directly revolve around behaviors, and it is also true that there is always a social aspect to moral choices. However, it is misleading to depict morality as exclusively an issue of a body of social norms and behaviors, since such a conception removes the voluntary aspect of the individual from the moral situation. It is clear that societies do develop moral codes, and that such codes are often dominant in the determination of an individual's behavior. However, these historical and sociological conclusions should not hide the fact that the ultimate sense of the moral sphere is of an aspect of human life in which the mature individual, whatever society and social tradition he may be rooted in, freely chooses a code of norms and behaviors. That is, "morality" and "moral," philosophically speaking, are not simply rooted in adherence to imposed social norms.

We have, then, two senses of morality: one, *formal* or *philosophical,* referring to a certain sphere or type of experience; and a second, *contextual* or *social,* referring to specific norms and behaviors. The link between these two senses is that the social sense of morality refers to particular norms and behaviors prescribed by a society for a certain type of situation, while the philosophic sense of morality refers to the nature of the moral situation itself, devoid of reference to any particular set of social norms or responses. The sociological conception alone is one-sided because it implies that morality is exclusively a question of adherence to a certain social code. The philosophical view in itself is equally misleading if understood as meaning that morality is exclusively a matter of individual contemplation and/or choice without any reference to one's social context. Taken together, these two perspectives provide a more balanced picture of the moral sphere.

This common assumption also stands in marked contrast to the conventional assumption of many traditional and contemporary programs of moral education. The conventional assumption is that morality is a specific set of values and behaviors to be transmitted to the young, and that moral education is one of the primary vehicles for such transmission. The sign of success in moral education, then, becomes the student's ability to reproduce verbally and behaviorally the transmitted moral values and behaviors. The second common assumption of moral philosophy, however, contradicts the conventional assumption, implying that moral education is as much involved with the teaching of *the art* of morality as it is with the transmission of a specific set of moral values.

3. A third common assumption of moral philosophy deals with the importance of *moral principles* to the moral sphere (and hence to moral education). According to this assumption, moral principles constitute

an indispensable component of the moral life and hence of moral education. This does not mean, of course, that there is unanimity in moral philosophy vis-à-vis the nature of any particular moral principle as *the* moral principle. Instead, what we are saying is that a central theme of moral philosophy is the belief that the moral sphere is not totally local, private, or unique, but rather has certain general characteristics and therefore can potentially and logically be governed by one or more generalizable principles. (Even the existentialist moral position postulates a cardinal and generally applicable principle; see Chapter 7). This means that in morality a person is not simply choosing between norms and behaviors at particular moments, but is also choosing principles which will guide his own and others' norms and behaviors in all such similar situations in the future.

We must, however, emphasize the qualification already noted: there is among moral philosophers far greater agreement on the *importance* of moral principles to moral life than on their specific *form* and *nature*. On the latter subject there is a wide range of divergent opinions. For example, one position argues that moral principles are Divine dictates or declarations and hence, *sui generis,* Good or Right, thereby implying a notion of moral education as training for adherence to such dictates. A more modified religious position (as exemplified by the Phenix selection in this volume, Chapter 4) might argue that the validity of moral principles lies not in their Divine origin, but in their "rationality and human value." In such a case moral education would be less concerned with inculcating and educating for adherence to such principles *per se* than with indicating and defending the validity and value of such principles for human existence. A social notion of the moral principle would argue that such statements are binding directives for behavior within particular societies; moral education would then become socialization on the basis of such principles. This position is close to the traditional religious position described above, in that both regard moral principles as established and binding statements. The only difference between the two positions is the conception of the origin and binding force behind the principles. A fourth conception regards moral principles as arbitrary dictates of the state or as external suppressions of human society.[5] Such an argument admits of the existence and the in-

[5]See S. Freud, *Civilization and Its Discontents* (New York: W. W. Norton and Company, 1961), pp. 42-45, 89.

fluence of such principles in human life, but it claims that such influence is destructive and anti-human and hence not necessarily "really
moral." A fifth position regards a moral principle as a prescriptive statement which expresses and guides potential choices in moral situations.[6]
According to this position, the moral principle is not *a priori* binding
or "true"; rather, it is one guide to human behavior, which only becomes
binding when the individual accepts it and becomes bound by it. In this
view, the fact of its existence as a moral principle does not in itself make
such a principle "true," "valid," or "binding." Moral principles are
taken only to be statements of potential alternatives until that moment
when the agent turns the statement into a binding principle by accepting
it and acting upon it. In this sense, the moral agent does, in fact, "create"
his own moral principles.

The most obvious implication of the centrality of the moral principle to moral life is that moral education must be principled education;
i.e., it is an education whose contents include principles, and whose objectives encompass the development of agents who can act on principles.
Thus, moral education is not simply skill training in how to act in certain ways, but rather must include provision for preparation to understand and apply principles to relevant situations in human existence. It
is also true, however, that the nature of moral education programs is very
much defined by the respective notion of the moral principle or principles accepted. The contents, methods, and objectives of moral education will very much depend on whether the moral principle is assumed
to be Divine truth, social law, anti-social dictate, or suggestive guide.
Once again, the careful clarification of underlying assumptions becomes
decisive for the successful implementation of programs of moral education.

Common Problems

We turn now to what will be called "common problems" of moral
philosophy as they represent *constellations of problems and issues* which
are central both to moral philosophy and to the understanding and explication of the tasks of moral education. In this case, moral philosophy

[6]See R. M. Hare: *The Language of Morals* (London: Oxford University
Press, 1952), and *Freedom and Reason* (London: Oxford University Press,
1963).

is less clear in giving explicit answers to essential questions than it is in highlighting the crucial questions.

1. The first common problem of moral philosophy has to do with the constellation of issues related to the role of *reasoning* in ethics. The essential question here is: Do reasoning and reasons play *any* role in moral decision-making, and if so, to what extent? One prominent trend in moral philosophy has been concerned with giving an affirmative answer to this question and hence with carving out some theory of reasoning in ethics.[7] In such a case the philosophic task is to clearly delineate the extent and nature of reasoning in ethics. Such a task has usually been undertaken on the basis of the assumption that reasoning and reasons do play some role in ethics but that they are by no means the sole or even the central determinants in moral judgements and moral decision-making.

Actual philosophic discussions of moral reasoning have usually encompassed three sorts of activities.[8] The first is examination of the concept "reasoning" to show that the term itself does not refer to an obscure metaphysical phenomenon, but rather simply denotes a procedure of bringing to bear on phenomena explanations, supportive evidence, and justifications. Thus, the terms "reasons" and "reasoning" are sometimes preferred over "reason" or "Reason," since the latter has connotations of *a* unique metaphysical procedure. "Reasoning" emphasizes the process notion, and "reasons" the idea of alternative forms of justification. The thrust of this type of discussion, then, is to show that moral reasoning *is* like other forms of reasoning in the sense that it refers to procedures of judgement and decision-making based on supportive evidence.

However, there is a reluctance to say that the nature of the decision-making process and of supportive evidence in the moral sphere is exactly like other reasoning, especially the scientific. Thus, a second aspect of the philosophic discussion of reasoning in ethics is analysis of the nature of science, in order to point out the similarities and differences between it and the moral sphere. The objective of the moral philosopher in such cases is to preserve the validity of reasoning in the moral sphere but to show how it differs from the scientific notion of reasoning. A third

---

[7]There are also, of course, positions which reject any notion of reason in ethics; see Frankena, *Ethics*, pp. 88-92.

[8]A good example of a philosophic discussion of reasoning in ethics encompassing these three activities is Toulmin's *The Place of Reason in Ethics*.

prominent aspect of the philosophic discussion of moral reasoning is analysis of the nature of moral reasoning itself as a unique phenomenon. The objective of such discussion is to describe the nature of the moral situation and to show the specific and unique role and functioning of reasons and reasoning in such a situation.

With reference to the issue of moral reasoning, the problems and procedures of moral philosophy are as important for moral education as are the specific philosophic answers offered. That is, it is mandatory that any theory and practice of moral education be rooted in some position vis-à-vis the role of reason in ethics. Second, such a theory and practice must reflect a clear conception of the similarities and differences between moral and scientific reasoning. Finally, any program of moral education must be rooted in a fairly specific notion of the procedures of moral reasoning if it is to effectively take on the task of teaching the art of moral reasoning. In short, the theory and practice of moral education must deal with the very same problems (in this case, the role of reason in ethics) which have perplexed the moral philosopher. Further, it may be argued that one task of the moral educator is to expose the student to such central issues of moral philosophy as the question of reasoning in ethics and others raised in this volume. In other words, one of the tasks of moral education is to make the child a moral philosopher.

2. The second common problem of moral philosophy revolves around the issue of a *theory of moral value*. The point of this common problem is that any notion of "moral" is *a priori* linked to some concept of value ("good," "bad," "right," "wrong"), and hence any program of moral education must assume and reflect some theory of value. Once again, the tradition of moral philosophy encompasses a multitude of theories of value, from the Platonic notion of the Good to the Utilitarian's keystone principle of the greatest good for the greatest number. The analysis and discussion of alternative theories of moral value is, then, obviously of key importance to any theory and practice of moral education. Moral education programs do clearly reflect some underlying conceptions of the Good, and it becomes essential that such underlying assumptions be understood, agreed upon, and clearly posited. The heart of this common problem, then, is that there is no such thing as the moral sphere or the moral life (and, hence, no moral education) without a confrontation with the fundamental question of what is the best available and most acceptable theory of moral value.

Contemporary analytic moral philosophy adds an important so-phistication to discussions of theory of value—theory of the nature of "good"—and its link with moral education. Philosophers have noted that words like "good," "bad," "right," "wrong" do not always refer to a property or phenomenon, but rather are sometimes used to denote an evaluation or reaction by someone to properties or phenomena. That is, when words like "good" and "bad" are used, they often function like a smile or nod of the head, or like moans, groans, or sighs, rather than as descriptive terms. In addition, language analysts have noticed that words like "good" and "bad" are not simply verbal reactions to or evalu-ations of phenomena *per se,* but rather reactions to and evaluations of certain *types* of phenomena. That is, words like "good" and "bad" are used to refer to certain phenomena (e.g., giving, cheating, smoking) *and* to urge, opt for, or reject such phenomena. (Giving—yes! Cheating —no! Smoking—no! "I shouldn't smoke." "You shouldn't cheat." "We should all give of ourselves.") The point of this claim is that, regardless of whatever "good" or "bad" may mean, the words have a certain type of function and usage in the moral sphere beyond their meanings. Thus, the moral philosopher is concerned not only with the presentation of alternative theories of moral value but also with expositions of the way moral terms function in our common language.

The linguistic point is of great importance for moral education, whether it is taken as a rejection of certain naturalist theories of "good" or regarded simply as an additional contribution of moral philosophy to any theory or discussion of moral value. It is indeed obvious that people do talk about many things as "good" (or "bad" or "right" or "wrong") when there seems to be no common connection between the phenomena themselves. Cars, soda, clothes, boats, courses, books, hats, values, and behaviors are all called "good," and it is a sticky logical exercise to at-tempt to find the common denominator of these various things worthy of being called by the same "name." This fact is one of the major con-fusions in the moral sphere. The individual concerned with the nature of "morality" and desirous of living "the Good life" is promptly bom-barded with a host of "goods" which seem to have no logic of their own. The linguistic analysis of "good" can contribute to the clarification of this confusion and to a more precise delineation of the moral from the non-moral sphere. Thus, moral philosophy is essential to moral edu-cation both in terms of projecting alternative theories of the moral good and at the same time in terms of clarifying some of the peculiarities of ordinary moral language.

THE LIMITS OF MORAL PHILOSOPHY'S CONTRIBUTION

A discussion of the relationship of moral philosophy to moral education must not only discuss the extent of the potential philosophic contribution, but also its limits. Moral philosophy is only *one* contributory source for the development of a theory and practice of moral education, and thus it is essential to have a clear picture of the scope and boundaries of its potential contribution.

First, moral philosophy cannot *prove* what is good or right, or *show* exactly how one justifies all moral choices, or *point* to the proper role of reasoning in ethics. The most moral philosophy can do is to clarify alternative positions on such issues and to argue for one position rather than another. This means that the moral educator cannot simplistically determine whether a certain program of moral education is "good" or "bad," "right" or "wrong," by consulting with the moral philosopher. All the moral philosopher can do in such cases is to clarify the underlying assumptions of particular programs and indicate whether the practical program is consistent with those assumptions.

Second, moral philosophy cannot provide statistical measurements of the moral life of particular societies, since it is not equipped with the appropriate methodology for such measurement. For example, moral philosophy cannot indicate what percentage of the population regards tax evasion as bad, or adultery as permissible, if undetected. Moreover, the moral philosopher probably would not be influenced by such reports if they were made available. Similarly, moral philosophy cannot measure the impact of youth culture on the transmission of moral values. And moral philosophy cannot measure the success of moral education programs in conveying the moral values of the particular society. Tasks of this sort are rooted in careful observation of social life and behavior in particular contexts, in measurements of such life and behavior, and in statistical computation in terms of particular societies. These are tasks for which social science and especially sociology are uniquely equipped.

Third, moral philosophy cannot describe the chronological and psychological moral development of children; that is the domain of psychology. Moral philosophy is not methodologically equipped to observe and measure attitudes and behaviors at different stages of development and then to make appropriate generalizations. Moral philosophy can only elucidate the particular conception of "moral" or "morality" assumed and studied in a particular psychological system (e.g., "moral" referring to virtues, as per Hartshorne and May, or "moral" applied to thinking, as per Kohlberg); it cannot, however, perform the empirical study.

Fourth, moral philosophy cannot develop specific pedagogic principles for the practice of moral education in a specific time and place, since the process of developing operative educational principles and practices is related to a host of factors, only one of which is moral philosophy. Such a process includes the contributions of moral philosophy but also must take into account the contributions of sociology, anthropology, and psychology, as well as the realities of the particular educational situation, the nature of the teaching staff, the nature of the curriculum, and the particular moral values of the school and the society. Thus, it would be illusory to assume that moral philosophy is *the* determinant factor of an effective moral education program. The contribution of the moral philosopher is to bring the moral philosophic method and tradition to bear on issues of moral education. It is also, perhaps, to contribute to the synthesis of various other contributions in order to produce an operative and testable theory of moral education. And it is to provide the moral educator with a sophisticated perspective on the difficult task he would try to perform.

We hope it is clear that we believe that there are no easy answers to the philosophical and pedagogical questions of moral education. It is this fact which makes the subject both frustrating and fascinating at the very same time. Because of the complexity of the moral sphere, any attempt to oversimplify these domains would be both mischievous and misleading. Nevertheless, if a society establishes the moral life as a priority, then it is compelled to deal with it in the same way that it deals with other top priority issues. The complexity of the moral sphere, then, is not an excuse for superficial treatment or neglect of this subject. The moral philosopher has an important role to play in insuring the sophistication and depth necessary to the serious consideration of moral education. "His is not the task to complete," but he certainly has a key and crucial role in the identification of the central issues of moral existence. It is such a function, then, which defines the subject and purpose of this volume.

PART ONE *Morality*
and Philosophy

We have argued that moral philosophy is of great importance for a clear understanding of the issues of the theory and practice of moral education. In our General Introduction we examined some of the substantive contributions of moral philosophy to the realities of moral education. In Part One we shall focus more carefully on the nature of the domain of moral philosophy and on its treatment of moral problems.

William Frankena's discussion of "morality and moral philosophy" is a concise introduction to the issues moral philosophers talk about and the ways in which they approach their task. In this selection Frankena introduces key terms in the language of moral philosophy, catalogs its key contents, and demonstrates its characteristic method of dealing with those contents. This selection by its example clarifies the distinction we discussed in the General Introduction, between "moralizing" and "moral philosophy." Frankena is not "moralizing": he is not concerned with the evaluation or criticism of norms and behaviors of contemporary American society, or with the prescription of new value orientations for that society. Rather, his objective is to present a map of that sphere of thinking called moral philosophy.

The second and third chapters of this section are not concerned with the meta-activity of *analyzing* the nature of moral philosophy but rather with the explication of central aspects of the moral domain. Soltis' article may be regarded as a continuation and expansion of Frankena's introductory discussion of the nature of morality. His objective is to analyze the meaning of morality by focusing on common language usages of the term "morality" and especially on the fact that the term is seen to be used exclusively in human contexts. The fact that men and not machines can be "moral" is the opening wedge he uses in his attempt to get us to focus more precisely on the *nature* of the moral sphere. An important methodological aspect of this analysis is the assumption that the very language used to talk about morality is a key to the basic clarification of what we take to be included and excluded from the moral sphere. Once again, Soltis' article is an example of philosophic clarification and explication of key concepts of the language of morality, rather than a prescription of how men should behave or what they should believe.

In the third chapter, taking up Soltis' challenge to clearly delineate the moral sphere, Chazan attempts to present a comprehensive picture of the situation denoted as "moral." His concern is to develop a formal framework which distinguishes the moral from the non-moral situation. It is important to note that the concern in this case is not with the moral versus the immoral, or the "good" versus the "bad," but simply with those characteristics which define a situation, in a descriptive sense, as "moral." Unless we know what is to count as "moral" in this sense, it would be most difficult to talk intelligently about or to make plans for moral education.

The first section, then, sets the scene. First, it introduces the domain in which we shall operate, as well as the manner in which the issues of moral philosophy and moral education will be approached. Second, the reader is introduced to those key components of the moral situation which become the subjects of more detailed analysis in the ensuing chapters.

I

*Morality and Moral Philosophy**
WILLIAM K. FRANKENA

Suppose that all your life you have been trying to be a good person, doing your duty as you see it and seeking to do what is for the good of your fellowmen. Suppose, also, that many of your fellowmen dislike you and what you are doing and even regard you as a danger to society, although they cannot really show this to be true. Suppose, further, that you are indicted, tried, and condemned to death by a jury of your peers, all in a manner which you correctly consider to be quite unjust. Suppose, finally, that while you are in prison awaiting execution, your friends arrange an opportunity for you to escape and go into exile with your family. They argue that they can afford the necessary bribes and will not be endangered by your escaping; that if you escape, you will enjoy a longer life; that your wife and children will be better off; that your friends will still be able to see you; and that people generally will think that you should escape. Should you take the opportunity?

An Example of Ethical Thinking (Socrates)

This is the situation Socrates, the patron saint of moral philosophy, is in at the opening of Plato's dialogue, the *Crito*. The dialogue gives us

*Reprinted with permission of the publisher from *Ethics,* by William K. Frankena (Englewood Cliffs, N. J.: Prentice-Hall, Inc., 1963), pp. 1-10. Copyright © 1963.

his answer to our question and a full account of his reasoning in arriving at it. It will, therefore, make a good beginning for our study. Socrates first lays down some points about the approach to be taken. (1) We must not let our decision be affected by our emotions, but must examine the question and follow the best reasoning. We must try to get our facts straight and to keep our minds clear. Questions like this can and should be settled by reason. (2) We cannot answer such questions by appealing to what people generally think. They may be wrong. We must try to find an answer we ourselves can regard as correct. We must think for ourselves. (3) We ought never to do what is morally wrong. The only question we need answer is whether what is proposed is right or wrong, not what will happen to us, what people will think of us, or how we feel about what has happened.

Having said this, Socrates goes on to give, in effect, a threefold argument to show that he ought not to break the laws by escaping. (1) We ought never to harm anyone. Socrates' escaping would harm the state, since it would violate and show disregard for the state's laws. (2) If one remains living in a state when one could leave it, one tacitly agrees to obey its laws; hence, if Socrates were to escape he would be breaking an agreement, which is something one should not do. (3) One's society or state is virtually one's parent and teacher, and one ought to obey one's parents and teachers.

In each of these arguments Socrates appeals to a general moral rule or principle which, upon reflection, he and his friend Crito accept as valid: (1) that we ought never to harm anyone, (2) that we ought to keep our promises, and (3) that we ought to obey or respect our parents and teachers. In each case he also uses another premise which involves a statement of fact and applies the rule or principle to the case in hand: (1) If I escape I will do injury to society, (2) if I escape I will be breaking a promise, and (3) if I escape I will be disobeying my parent and teacher. Then he draws a conclusion about what he should do in his particular situation. This is a typical pattern of reasoning in moral matters and is nicely illustrated here.

It happens that Socrates thinks his three principles all lead to the same conclusion. But sometimes when two or more rules apply to the same case, this is not true. In fact, most moral problems arise in situations where there is a "conflict of duties," that is, where one moral principle pulls one way and another pulls the other way. Socrates is represented in Plato's *Apology* as saying that if the state spares his life on condition that he no longer teach as he has been doing he will not obey, because (4) he has been assigned the duty of teaching by the god, Apollo, and (5) his teaching is necessary for the true good of the state. He would then be involved in a conflict of duties. His duty to obey the state applies, but so do two other duties, (4) and (5), and these he judges to take precedence over his duty to obey the commands of the state. Here, then, he resolves the problem, not just by appealing to rules, for this is not enough, but by deciding which rules take precedence over which others. This is another typical pattern of reasoning in ethics.

To return to the *Crito,* Socrates completes his reasoning by answering his friend's arguments in favor of escaping by contending that he will not really be doing himself, his friends, or even his family any good by becoming an outlaw and going into exile; he also asserts that death is not an evil to an old man who has done his best, whether there is a hereafter or not. In other words, he maintains that there are no good moral grounds on the other side and no good prudential ones—which would count only if moral considerations were not decisive—either.

All this is interesting because it illustrates two kinds of moral problems and how one reflective and serious moral agent went about solving them. It also shows us much of Socrates' working ethics: principles (1) to (5) plus the second-order principle that (4) and (5) take precedence over the duty to obey the state. This duty to obey the state, by the way, is for him a *derivative* rule which rests on (1), (2), and (3), which are more *basic.* One can find out one's own working ethics by seeing how one would answer these two problems oneself, or others like them. This is a good exercise. Suppose that in doing this you disagree with Socrates' answer to the *Crito* problem. You might then challenge his principles, which Crito did not do. You might ask Socrates to justify his regarding (1), (2), and (3) as valid, and Socrates would have to try to answer you, since he believes in reason and argument in ethics, and wants knowledge, not just true opinion.

At this point Socrates might argue that (2), for example, is valid because it follows from a still more basic principle, say, (4) or (5). That is, he might maintain that we should keep promises because it is commanded by the gods or because it is necessary for the general welfare. But, of course, you might question his more basic principle, if you have any good reason for doing so (if you question without reason, you are not really entering into the dialogue). At some point you or he will almost inevitably raise the question of how ethical principles, especially the most *basic* ones, are to be justified anyway; and this is likely to lead to the further question of what is meant by saying that something is right, good, virtuous, just, and the like, a question which Socrates in fact often raises in other dialogues. (In the *Euthyphro*, for example, he argues, in effect, that "right" does not mean "commanded by the gods.")

The Nature of Ethics or Moral Philosophy

When this happens this discussion has developed into a full-fledged philosophical one. Ethics is a branch of philosophy; it is *moral philosophy* or philosophical thinking about morality, moral problems, and moral judgments. What this involves is illustrated by the sort of thinking Socrates was doing in the *Crito* and *Apology,* supplemented as we have supposed it to be. Such philosophical thinking will now be explained more fully.

Moral philosophy arises when, like Socrates, we pass beyond the stage in which we are directed by traditional rules and even beyond the stage in which these rules are so internalized that we can be said to be inner-directed, to the stage in which we think for ourselves in critical and general terms (as the Greeks were beginning to do in Socrates' day) and achieve a kind of autonomy as moral agents. We may, however, distinguish three kinds of thinking which relate to morality in one way or another.

1. There is descriptive empirical inquiry, historical or scientific, such as is done by anthropologists, historians, psychologists, and sociologists. Here, the goal is to describe or explain the phenomena of morality or to work out a theory of human nature which bears on ethical questions.

2. There is normative thinking of the sort that Socrates was doing in the *Crito* or that anyone does who asks what is right, good, or obligatory. This may take the form of asserting a normative judgment like

"I ought not to try to escape from prison,"

"Knowledge is good," or

"It is always wrong to harm someone,"

and giving or being ready to give reasons for this judgment. Or it may take the form of debating with oneself or with someone else about what is good or right in a particular case or as a general principle, and then forming some such normative judgments as a conclusion.

3. There is also "analytical," "critical," or "meta-ethical" thinking. This is the sort of thinking we imagined that Socrates would have come to if he had been challenged to the limit in the justification of his normative judgments. He did, in fact, arrive at this sort of thinking in other dialogues. It does not consist of empirical or historical inquiries and theories, nor does it involve making or defending any normative or value judgments. It does not try to answer either particular or general questions about what is good, right, or obligatory. It asks and tries to answer logical, epistemological, or semantical questions like the following: What is the meaning or use of the expressions "(morally) right" or "good"? How can ethical and value judgments be established or justified? Can they be justified at all? What is the nature of morality? What is the distinction between the moral and the nonmoral? What is the meaning of "free" or "responsible"?

Many recent moral philosophers limit ethics or moral philosophy to thinking of the third kind, excluding from it all questions of psychology and empirical science and also all normative questions about what is good or right. In this book, however, we shall take the more traditional view of our subject. We shall take ethics to include meta-ethics as just described, but as also including normative ethics or thinking of the second kind, though only when this deals with general questions about what is good or right and not when it tries to solve particular problems as Socrates was mainly doing in the *Crito*. In fact, we shall take ethics to be primarily concerned with providing the general outlines of a normative theory to help us in answering problems about what is right or ought to be done, and as being interested in meta-ethical questions mainly because it seems necessary to answer such questions before one can be entirely satisfied with one's normative theory (although ethics is also interested in meta-ethical questions for their own sakes). However, since certain psychological and anthropological theories are considered to have a bearing on the answers to normative and meta-ethical questions, as we shall see in discussing egoism, hedonism, and relativism, we shall also include descriptive or empirical thinking of the first kind.

The Nature of Morality

We have described ethics as philosophy which is concerned with *morality* and its problems and judgments, or with *moral* problems and judgments. Now the terms "moral" and "ethical" are often used as equivalent to "right" or "good" and as opposed to "immoral" and "unethical." But we also speak of moral problems, moral judgments, moral codes, moral arguments, moral experiences, the moral consciousness, or the moral point of view. "Ethical" is used in this way too. Here "ethical" and "moral" do not mean "morally right" or "morally good." They mean "pertaining to morality" and are opposed to the "*non*moral" or "*non*ethical," not to the "*im*moral" or "*un*ethical." Similarly, the term "morality" is sometimes used as opposed to "immorality," as when we say that the essence of morality is love or speak of the morality of an action. But we also use the word "morality" to refer to something which is coordinate with but different from art, science, law, convention, or religion, though it may be related to them. This is the way we use the term when we ask, "What is morality? How does it differ from law? How is it related to religion?" In this sense "morality" means what Bishop Butler called "the moral institution of life." This is how I have been using "morality" and propose to go one using it. Correspondingly, I shall use "moral" and "ethical" in this sense also.

Now, morality in the sense indicated is, in one aspect, a social enterprise, not just a discovery or invention of the individual for his own guidance. Like one's language, state, or church, it exists before the individual, who is inducted into it and becomes more or less of a participant in it, and it goes on existing after him. Moreover, it is not social merely in the sense of being a system governing the relations of one individual to others; such a system might still be entirely the individual's own construction, as some parts of one's code of action with respect to others almost inevitably are, for example, "My rule is to smile first." Morality, of course, is social in this sense to a large extent; however, it is also social in its origins, sanctions, and functions. It is an instrument of society as a whole for the guidance of individuals and smaller groups. It makes demands on individuals which are, initially at least, external to them. Even if the individuals become spokesmen of these demands, as they usually do to some extent through what is called "internalization," the demands are still not merely theirs nor directed only at themselves. If they come to disagree with the demands, then, as Socrates thought and as we shall see later, they must still do so from the moral point of view which has somehow been inculcated into them. One may think of society, as many people do, as having a supernatural dimension and as including a divine lawgiver, but even then one must ascribe this social character to morality.

As such a social institution, morality must be contrasted with prudence. It may be that prudence and morality dictate some of the same conduct, for example, honesty. It may also be that prudence is a moral virtue; however, it is not characteristic of the moral point of view to determine what is right or virtuous wholly in terms of what the individual desires or of what is to his interest. In Freudian terms, morality and prudence are both attempts to regulate the id; but while prudence is simply a function of the reality-principle in the ego, morality is the function of a super-ego which does not think merely in terms of getting what is desired by the individual id or even in terms of salvaging the greatest balance of satisfaction over frustration for it.

As a social system of regulation, morality is like law on the one hand and convention or etiquette on the other. All of these systems are social in a way in which prudence is not, and some of the same expressions are used in all of them, for example, the words "right" and "should." But convention does not deal with matters of such crucial social importance as those dealt with by law and morality; it seems to rest largely on considerations of appearance, taste, and convenience. Thus, morality is distinguished from convention by certain features which it shares with law; similarly, it is also distinguished from law (with which it overlaps, for example, in forbidding murder) by certain features which it shares with convention, namely, in not being created or changeable by anything like a deliberate legislative, executive, or judicial act, and in having as its sanctions, not physical force or the threat of it but, at most, praise and blame and other such mainly verbal signs of favor and disfavor. Some writers have even held that the only proper motives or sanctions for morality are purely internal ones like the sentiment of benevolence or the desire to do what is right for its own sake; there is much to be said for this view, even if it hardly describes the whole practical working of morality. At least it highlights the fact that physical force and certain kinds of prudential considerations do not strictly belong to the idea of a moral institution of life.

However, morality, at least as it has developed in the western world, also has a more individualistic or protestant aspect. As Socrates implied and recent philosophers have stressed (perhaps too much), morality fosters or even calls for the use of reason and for a kind of autonomy on the part of the individual, asking him, when mature and normal, to make his own decisions, though possibly with someone's advice, and even stimulating him to think out the principles or goals in the light of which he is to make his decisions. Morality is a social institution of life, but it is one which promotes rational self-guidance or self-determination in its members. In Matthew Arnold's words, it asks us to be ". . . self-govern'd, at the feet of Law."

Accordingly, it has been usual for moral philosophers to distinguish stages of morality, which can be more or less clearly traced both in the history of our culture and in the life of the individual, to distinguish, for instance (a) "pre-rational," "customary," or "group" morality and (b) "personal," "rational," or "reflective" morality. Improving on this in an interesting and instructive way, David Riesman, a social scientist, has recently portrayed four moral or social types in *The Lonely Crowd:*

1. The tradition-directed individual and/or society.
2. The inner-directed individual and/or society.
3. The other-directed individual and/or society.
4. The autonomous individual and/or society.

The general idea here, and in much recent social psychology and moral philosophy, is that morality starts as a set of culturally defined goals and of rules governing achievement of the goals, which are more or less external to the individual and imposed on him or inculcated as habits. These goals and rules may and generally do, at least to some extent, become "internalized" or "interiorized," that is, the individual takes them as his own and regulates his own conduct by them; he develops a "conscience" or "superego." This process of internalization may be quite irrational but, as we shall see, it is typical for morality to accompany its inculcations with at least a modicum of reason-giving. Thus, we (and even the Navaho) tend to give reasons with our moral instructions as soon as the child has attained an age at which he is capable of something like discretion, and we even lead him to feel that it is appropriate to ask for reasons. That is why it seemed appropriate to Socrates, at his juncture in the history of Greece, to ask for definitions and arguments in matters of morals.

We may then, without leaving the moral fold, move from a rather irrational kind of inner direction to a more rational one in which we achieve an examined life and a kind of autonomy, become moral agents on our own, and may even reach a point when we can criticize the rules and values of our society, as Socrates did in the *Apology* and the *Crito* Some find too much anxiety in this transition and try to "escape from freedom" in one way or another (including other-direction), some apparently can make the transition only with the help of psychoanalysis, but for others it involves no major difficulties other than the use of some hard thought such as Socrates engaged in.

Clearly, it is in the last stages of this process that moral philosophy plays its natural role. We are then—or from now on may imagine ourselves to be—in the middle or later states of the moral life as these were just outlined. It is the thinking to be done here that we mainly wish to help on its way, although we also hope, in spite of the element of danger involved, to pull those who are not so far along out of their unreflective nest and its dogmatic slumber.

Factors in Morality

The institution of morality contains a number of factors: (1) certain *forms of judgment* in which *particular* objects are said to have or not to have a certain moral quality, obligation, or responsibility; (2) the implication that it is appropriate and possible to give *reasons* for these judgments; (3) some *rules, principles, ideals,* and *virtues* which can be expressed in more *general judgments* and which form the background against which particular judgments are made and reasons given for them; (4) certain characteristic natural or acquired *ways of feeling* which accompany these judgments, rules, and ideals, and help to move us to act in accordance with them; (5) certain *sanctions* or additional sources of motivation which are also often expressed in verbal judgments, namely, holding responsible, praising, and blaming; (6) a *point of view* which is taken in all this judging, reasoning, and feeling, and which is somehow different from those taken in prudence, art, and the like. For our purposes, we may center most of our discussion on the moral judgments which are involved in factors (1), (2), and (5). These have a central place in morality, and the main questions of normative ethics and meta-ethics relate to them.

Kinds of Moral Judgment

Moral or ethical judgments are of various kinds. As has been indicated, they may be particular or general. They may also be stated in different persons and tenses. These differences are all important in their places, but here we must stress another difference. In some of our moral judgments, we say that a certain action or kind of action is morally right, wrong, obligatory, a duty, or ought or ought not to be done. In others we talk, not about actions or kinds of action, but about persons, motives, intentions, traits of character, and the like, and we say of them that they are morally good, bad, virtuous, vicious, responsible, blameworthy, saintly, despicable, and so on. In these two kinds of judgment, the things talked about are different and what is said about them is different. (We do also speak of "good actions" or "deeds," but here "good" is not properly used as a synonym of "right," as it often is; properly used, it seems to mean either that the action has a good motive or that it has good consequences.) I shall call the former *judgments of moral obligation* and the latter *judgments of moral value*.

There are also *judgments of nonmoral value*, which I shall usually call simply "value judgments." In these we evaluate, not so much actions, persons, motives, and the like, but all sorts of other things: cars, paintings, experiences, forms of government, and what not. We say they are good, bad, desirable, undesirable, and so on, but we do not mean that they are morally good or morally bad, since they are generally not the kinds of things that can be morally good or bad. A study of these judgments is not, as such, a part of ethics or moral philosophy. But since it will turn out that a consideration of what is good (nonmorally) is involved in determining what is morally right or wrong, we must include a discussion of such value judgments.

We obtain, then, the following outline of the kinds of *normative judgment* that are of interest to us:

I. Ethical or moral judgments.

    A. Judgments of moral obligation.

        1. Particular, e.g. (assuming terms are used in their moral senses),
            a. I ought not to escape from prison now.
            b. You should become a missionary.
            c. What he did was wrong.

        2. General, e.g.,
            a. We ought to keep our agreements.
            b. Love is the fulfillment of the moral law.
            c. All men have a right to freedom.

B. Judgments of moral value.

   1. Particular, e.g.,

      a. My grandfather was a good man.

      b. Xavier was a saint.

      c. He is responsible for what he did.

      d. You deserve to be punished.

      e. Her character is admirable.

      f. His motive was good.

   2. General, e.g.,

      a. Benevolence is a virtue.

      b. Jealousy is an ignoble motive.

      c. Only a saint could forgive such carelessness.

      d. The ideally good man does not drink or smoke.

II. Judgments of nonmoral value, e.g.,

   A. That is a good car.

   B. Pleasure is good in itself.

   C. Miniver Cheevy did not have a very good life.

   D. Democracy is the best form of government.

In *normative ethics* we try primarily to arrive at a set of acceptable judgments (1) of moral obligation, (2) of moral value, and secondarily (3) of nonmoral value. In *meta-ethics* we mainly seek to work out a theory of the meaning and justification (1) of judgments of moral obligation, (2) of judgments of moral value, and also (3) of judgments of nonmoral value....

II

Men, Machines, and Morality*
JONAS F. SOLTIS

By use of some fairly simple-minded contrasts between machines and men, I would like to try to present what has become for me a most perplexing problem regarding the boundaries of the sphere of morality. In a preliminary way, however, I must admit that, as I stand here before the bar of mid-twentieth century technology, I willingly and knowingly plead guilty to the charge of having a nineteenth century conception of "machine." However, I beg to be excused for this "crime" because I merely wish to use the following "machine" examples to point to what I take to be some rather ordinary human assumptions about the sphere of morality which seem to be independent of any particular concept of "machine" or "Man." For example, I would expect fairly universal agreement that it makes no sense to refer to a machine as either moral or immoral. But positively, in all likelihood we would classify machines *qua* machines as non-moral or amoral things just as we generally refrain from ascribing morality to any non-human thing. Of course, I do not mean to imply that a machine cannot be *used* morally or immorally. But in such cases a machine is taken to be an instrument and not an agent in the same way as a gun placed in evidence at a murder trial is not on trial for *its* life while than man who wielded it is.

*Reprinted with permission of the publisher from *Philosophy of Education 1966*, F. T. Villemain, ed. (Edwardsville, Ill.: Philosophy of Education Society, 1966), pp. 15-19.

If I am correct about this omission of machines from the moral sphere, then it may be instructive to compare machines with men in an attempt to isolate those characteristics which provide good reasons for calling some of the actions of one moral and the other not. Naturally, the similarities will be of less interest than the differences. Psychological machine-like descriptions of man's internal parts are not ordinarily taken to be relevant to morality. Nor, I would argue, are strict behavioristic interpretations of human behavior which seem to say, "Push this button (stimulus) and you will get this result (response)." The ideas of mechanical cause and effect and automatic action seem to have little relevance to the moral sphere though both are shared in the man-machine universe of discourse. Thus, where man and machines are most similar or taken to be so, we find ourselves outside the moral sphere. But an important consideration coming out of this discussion is the clear fact that not all men's actions are within the moral sphere either (at least not those which are machine-like or mechanical) and so we can posit that the sphere of moral action for man is lesser than the total sphere of his actions.

But let us leave similarities and turn instead to some of the more obvious differences between men and machines which might be considered not only as distinguishing characteristics, but also as being most relevant to the moral dimension of man's activities. High on such list, I suppose, would be "freedom," the freedom to choose alternate courses of action or, indeed, to invent or create a novel course of action. Although I am taken by this claim, I have been advised by some of my 20th century machine-wise colleagues that modern machines are made which have this sort of freedom and flexibility built into them. Even if I didn't believe my colleagues, I do not find it logically impossible to imagine a machine with such freedom of choice, though I would still hesitate to call such a machine, or indeed any machine for that matter, a moral agent. So it seems that the quality of freedom of choice is at best a weakly arguable distinguishing feature and at worst, no mark at all for distinguishing between machines and men.

But there is also, of course, that whole area of human-ness called the "emotions" in which Hume and others saw the spring of moral action. Included here and obviously missing from machines are human feelings such as love, desire, commitment, duty, obligation, etc. More than the fact that man has the capacity for such feeling, there is his unique (or at least claimed to be so) ability to also be conscious of such feelings. I have no friends who claim feelings or consciousness for machines, but they are so enchanted by technological progress that they are unwilling to deny the possibility of a machine being invented which did have or at least displayed the overt signs of feeling and consciousness.

I trust, however, that most of you here would draw the line at this point and claim feeling and consciousness as unique qualities of the human "machine" alone. Even if this were so, however, I'm afraid that it would not bring us much closer to our goal of attempting to clearly delimit the moral sphere. For I (and I take it you recognize me as a man and not a machine) may have feelings which are non-moral (e.g. desire for respect from my colleagues) or feelings which may be moral, immoral, or amoral (e.g. love of wife, love of another's wife, love of fresh air).

But these examples display only the feelings of love and desire; what of those more special feelings usually tied directly to morality; those of commitment, duty, and obligation which I mentioned above? Perhaps these will fare better as markers for the boundaries of the moral sphere. Concerning commitment, one might feel *committed* to a life of scholarship, but this would not be generally treated as a moral commitment. Or with "duty," may I not be in poor health and yet feel it my *duty* to come to a PES conference, even though it would seem that my absence could hardly be considered immoral? And with "obligation," may I not feel obliged to stand when guests enter a room, and though I might be considered ill-mannered if I did not do so, I doubt that for that reason alone I would be considered immoral. So the having of feelings might provide us with an opening wedge between man and machine (and note I'm only willing to say might); nevertheless, we still fall short of delimiting the moral sphere.

There are, of course, other differences between machines and men which might be pointed to, but I have little hope that they will serve us any better to limit the moral sphere. So rather, at this juncture, I think that another tactic might more profitably be adopted. Instead of seeking what is unique about man over and against some machine counterpart, I will turn to the concept of "morality" itself to see if there are certain characteristics which will serve both to delimit the moral sphere and to separate men from machines or even perhaps show us how to make moral machines.

Along this line, it is interesting to note that a writer like Hare, who carefully examines the *Language of Morals*, spends most of his time with rules, commands, and principles of a non-moral sort (e.g. "shut the door") so that he may avoid the emotive quality of moral language. The point of interest for us here, however, is not his strategy but the assumption he makes which most of us would also adhere to—that some rules, commands, and principles are moral and some non-moral. In what remains of my time to speak, I will question this assumption by asking straightforwardly, "what makes a moral rule a *moral* rule?"

I think that we can all grant with Hare and other examiners of the *form* of moral language that there is no difference in form between the rule: "Do not walk on the grass" and the generally recognized moral rule "Do not commit adultery." If there is a difference, one would expect instead to find it in the *subject matter* and not in the form of the rule or command.

A number of candidates to discern moral from non-moral subject matter in such contexts come immediately to mind, but I think we will find that they will fall short of the mark of delimiting the moral sphere. Before examining these ideas, one ground rule (a logical and non-moral one) must be made clear, however. It would seem to me, at least, to be most improper to attempt to identify the moral sphere by pointing to those things (subject matters) which are already assumed to be moral. By that I mean that we cannot assume any *particular* substantive ethic and still impartially and objectively seek out the logical characteristics of rules which provide them with membership in the moral sphere, for by positing a particular substantive ethic, we already limit the moral sphere to whatever touches that ethic and all else falls outside of it. The problem I seek solution for, then is not what is "moral" assuming a particular ethic, but rather what, if anything, allows one to claim a rule is a moral rule without assuming some particular ethic. In a way this problem may be similar to the one faced by the anthropologist in the field who wishes to observe a culture and to report on its various institutions without allowing his views of his particular society, particular theological beliefs or particular morality to color his picture. In simple form, then, the ground rule I will operate on will be: *Do not count as a characteristic of the subject matter of a rule that which assumes some particular ethical view.* In a sense, all that I'm saying is that I would hope it to be possible to objectively set down a criterion for moral rules which will do the job of separating moral from non-moral rules generally for any society, time or place.

Having said this, I do not see any fault with counting as counter examples the general ideas we all hold in this time and place concerning certain substantive ethical positions. For as counter examples, their singular force against any universal criterion proposed is enough to deny the universal claimed.

But enough preliminaries; let us begin to test some idea. Let us assume that to be moral the subject matter of any rule must refer to *human conduct*. Then a rule whose subject matter refers to adulterous human conduct would have to be judged a moral rule while rules of algebra would be non-moral. But alas, so also would a rule have to be judged moral by this criterion which referred to the human conduct of walking on the grass or standing when guests enter the room.

Obviously, the catch-all mark of "pertaining to human conduct" is too broad, for it takes in any and every rule regarding human action from rules about walking on the grass or sipping one's soup to rules governing incest and murder. But there may be a partial clue in these simple examples, for in walking on the grass or in sipping one's soup, there is human conduct in relation to some *thing* (grass and soup) whereas in the case of incest and murder, there is a rule governing a relation between human and human, and not between a human and a thing. Without stretching too far, we could even bring suicide into this human relations area and so needn't even worry about self-related acts.

So our next candidate for a limiting criterion then could be given in some such form as the following: "To be judged a *moral* rule, the subject matter of the rule must deal with human conduct *as it relates to self or others.*" Although we have already seen the advantages of this added feature, it is unfortunate that it comes up short in such instances as rules which govern a game like football (with its rule about body contact with an opponent after the whistle has blown a play dead). Considering football players as sub-human will hardly get us out of this difficulty for we still have the rule governing human conduct between humans which says, "Stand whenever a guest or guests enter the room" (totally unnecessary if your guest is a machine, of course). Thus the limiting notion of human conduct and human relations in the purely human sphere is also too broad a criterion.

But surely there must be some prime candidate which I may have overlooked. Perhaps we could try some such as "The subject matter of a moral rule must be understood as *God-given*," but again obviously this would be of no aid in an atheistic society unless we would wish to deny the existence of moral rules in such a society, and that hardly seems proper. Even the idea of a rule whose underlying principle is humanity and respect of person is of no help if we allow that standing when a guest enters a room or tipping one's hat to a lady is based on the principle of respect for person or humanness.

Perhaps the time has come to seek the advice of an expert. William Frankena, the respected contemporary moral philosopher, has faced this very problem himself in his recent clear and readable little book on *Ethics*. There he also sees the need to distinguish between the nonmoral and the moral, but instead of looking at the subject matter of rules, as we have, he turns understandably to the identification of the different *objects* of moral and non-moral values. Values ascribed to "people, groups, traits, dispositions, emotions, motives, and intentions" mark moral values for Frankena while valuations of "experiences and forms of government . . ." (p. 48) belong to the non-moral sphere of valuation. To take his list, it certainly seems that he is at least half (that may be too generous, one quarter) right. In a moral sense we may judge *people* or *groups* as honest and hold morally dear the *trait* or *disposition* of honesty. The *emotion* of love for fellow man may be considered moral as may also be the *motive* of altruism or the *intent* of justice.

But, although an *experience* (as Frankena's object of non-moral value) may be judged non-morally as good in the sense of aesthetically pleasing or a *form of government* good in the sense of efficiency and flexibility, these same non-moral objects are likely candidates for the moral sphere. For instance, when we call democracy good we may very well mean *morally* good, the morally right form of government for man, or when we call communism evil we may very well mean morally evil, the immoral subjugation of man. Similarly experiences may be moral or immoral, as the law regarding "carnal experience of a minor" swiftly attests. So it seems at minimum that Frankena's candidates for exclusion from the moral sphere may on occasion enter into it.

But what of the true members, the first list of objects of moral values? Do they enjoy complete and unstinting membership? It hardly seems so. People may be judged good as, for instance, I might judge one of you to be a good scholar whose scholarship and person as a scholar I value highly while your morality makes me blush. Groups, obviously come in for similar treatment, but what of things like Frankena's "traits, dispositions, emotions, motives and intentions"? We may call the "trait" of patience a "virtue," but do we consider it a moral virtue? Even if we do, what of the trait of stubbornness?—it hardly seems to be a prime candidate for immorality! Having the disposition "to appreciate music" or "to be a pleasant person," seems equally non-moral. The emotion of fear of God or spiders may also be quite non-moral just as the motive or intention of the mountain climber to reach the top seems outside moral calculations while still able to be considered by some as a very "good" motive.

So it seems that even our expert Frankena fails us in that his objects of moral and non-moral values seem to be quite interchangeable and hence hardly will do as boundary markers for the sphere of morality. We could go to other experts, but again I suspect we have little hope for success. What then is the upshot of this discussion which gets nowhere? I can only answer for myself. In very personal terms, I can testify that I have wrestled with this problem well beyond the few ideas and examples I have offered to you here, and I find myself forced to reach the conclusion that unless some specific ethic is assumed, there seems to be no way to tell a moral rule or value from a non-moral rule or value.

Although I suspect that many of you who have patiently listened are quite eager to dissolve my problem with your wisdom or even with some simple idea I've overlooked, I feel obliged to go on just a bit more to indicate what I think this conclusion has to say to philosophers of education (just on the thin possibility that it may be a proper conclusion).

Although philosophers of education are noted for riding quite different and odd-looking horses, many have not been shy when it comes to mounting that pure white steed called "moral education" and galloping full speed into the forest of "prescriptions" and "programs" in search of the Promised Land of the Good Life and a Better World. Although I thus seem to caricature this enterprise and although I would expect to find few of you here with this particular bent, I think we can all agree that the contemporary world we live in could well profit from better moral training of the young and also that the possibility of such training is not totally eliminated from the realm of public education, nor the concerns of philosophers of education.

But the conclusion I've drawn from my search for the clear boundary markers for the sphere of morality (namely that unless some specific ethic is assumed, it is most difficult if not impossible to define such limits) leads me to suggest caution when approaching arguments or programs set forth as moral education. For if one argues for the need for moral education without assuming any particular ethic in his argument, then we are being given a rather empty, guide-line-less sphere of action to either accept or reject. On the other hand, we may be faced with an argument or program for moral education in *general* which does assume an ethic in *particular,* and then we should be aware of the two choices which confront us and not think we only have one. That is, we may accept the idea of the need for moral education while *rejecting* or *accepting* the particular brand of moral education being offered.

I would go one step further and say that any argument or program for moral education is empty unless it *does* assume some particular ethic, and then if it does, the fruitful point of contact for either acceptance or rejection is with regard to the assessment of the particular ethic involved and *not* with the *general* notion of moral education itself. Too many good men and good arguments, I fear, have been sidetracked by not focusing on the most relevant issue of the particular ethic involved in some brand of moral education being advocated. Who in his right mind could be against either mother or morals? It is only when we get down to the brass tacks of *which* mother and *which* morals that we have a legitimate focus for philosophical debates and judgments.

Quite obviously, we have moved in a very short time far from the initial comparison between machines and man to moral education and have not solved the thematic problem of this paper regarding the limits of the sphere of morality. If you will excuse the pun, however, I think there is a "moral" here. Even when philosophers fail to answer their unanswerable questions, what they do do may make the question clearer and may even make alternatives for practical action more easily discernible. To see that arguments for moral education *generally* are empty and that the real heart of the issue is in hidden particular ethical systems, is, for me at least, an advance of sorts. More broadly, I am even led to wonder if we in the 20th century haven't taken the sphere of morals to be too narrow and strayed from that ancient Greek notion of the full and complete "Good Life."

But that is another question hardly to be tackled at this point. Instead, I close with the invitation to you to help me solve my problem and to think about the essence of morality in objective logical terms and not, as I'm afraid we're all accustomed to, in personal, subjective, and particular terms.

III

The Moral Situation:
A Prolegomenon to Moral Education*
BARRY I. CHAZAN

One of the popular subjects of educational discourse is the relation of moral education to formal schooling. Is moral education a legitimate and central task of formal education, or is it exclusively a responsibility of the home and the church? Any such discussion of this topic and any relevant statement about moral education and the schools must be subjected to and evaluated in terms of two criteria, one logical and one educational. Such a statement must be *both* logically *and* educationally consistent. Let us, then, submit the three commonly held positions about the relation of moral education to formal education to this dual requirement.

One position about moral education and the schools holds that moral education is *not* a central concern of formal education and hence *need not* be seriously confronted in schools. This statement is logically valid, but educationally unacceptable. It is true that *if* moral education were not a central concern of formal education, *then* there would not be a need to confront it seriously. However, the educational premise of the statement—that moral education is *not* a central concern—is faulty. For the various objectives and enterprises of formal education *are directly related* to the moral sphere, whether so stated or not. If one refers to three commonly espoused goals of education—transmission

*Not previously published.

of a cultural heritage, training of the intellect, individual growth—it immediately becomes clear that each of these goals relates to faculties or agencies or qualities directly involved in moral behavior; e.g., society, the intellect, the total self. That is, the various activities of education (whatever the specific emphasis) *do* deal with moral education. Therefore, it is educationally impossible to divorce moral education from the general concerns of education. This first statement, then, is not helpful as a relevant guide to the theory and practice of moral education.[1]

A second position about moral education and the schools states that moral education *is* a central concern of education, but one *need not* seriously deal with it in formal education (this may well be the accepted and operative principle of moral education in practice). While this position may be educationally convenient and efficient, it is logically invalid. The premise of the position says that moral education *is* an important aspect of formal education, while the conclusion *denies* the importance of moral education in the practice of formal education. The conclusion does not at all follow from the premise, and is, in fact, contradictory to it. Thus, even if this statement *were* educationally acceptable, it is invalid as a statement about the theory and practice of moral education because it is illogical.

The third position on moral education is that moral education *is* a central concern of formal education and hence *must be* treated with rigor and seriousness. This statement is locically consistent, as the conclusion flows from the premise and does not contradict it . Educationally also, the statement is valid, since the premise is a statement reflecting an understanding of the nature of *all* the activities and processes involved in schooling. That is, this educational statement is consistent with the "givens" of the enterprise of formal education. This statement, then, is the only *logically and educationally* acceptable position about the relation of moral education to the formal school system, and it shall serve as the premise of the subsequent argument of this paper.

If it is true that moral education *is* a central concern of formal education and hence *must be* treated with rigor and seriousness, we must

---

[1]For two discussions dealing with the invalidity of this position, see: W. R. Niblett, ed., *Moral Principles in a Changing Society* (London: Faber and Faber, 1963); and R. S. Peters, *Ethics and Education* (London: George Allen and Unwin, Ltd., 1966).

then clarify the meaning of "seriously dealing with moral education." How does one confront the subject of moral education with rigor and seriousness?

The first step in such a confrontation is clarification of the subject of moral education. A clear understanding of the nature and content of moral education is crucial to any subsequent efforts to effect programs of moral education.

One apparently relevant source for such clarification would seem to be the history of moral education programs and materials in American education. A cursory review, however, reveals that traditional approaches to moral education have not been based on a total picture of the moral sphere, but have emphasized certain factors at the expense of others. For example, certain textbooks employed for the purpose of moral education have exclusively highlighted the *moral rule* as the essence of the moral situation.[2] The assumption behind such texts is that the (frequently rote) learning of moral rules is sufficient to guarantee desired moral attitudes and behaviors. A second approach to moral education, as embodied in some of the policy statements of public bodies and school systems, has been based on the realization that the learning of moral rules in itself does not guarantee moral behaviors, and that the task in moral education is to get the student to hold certain *attitudes* toward moral actions. Such programs have emphasized the developing of specific moral attitudes; e.g., love of neighbors, worth and dignity of the individual, brotherhood, charity.[3] A third position on moral education is based on the claim that *both* learning rules *and* developing attitudes are not enough. The real goal of moral education, according to this view, is to bring the student to *act* in certain desired ways: to see him translate his attitudes into behaviors. Programs in this vein (as, for example, the Kentucky Movement) have emphasized bus and cafe-

[2]*The New England Primer* (New York: Teachers College Press, 1962). See also, Ruth Elson, *Guardians of Tradition: Schoolbooks of the Nineteenth Century* (Lincoln: University of Nebraska Press, 1964).

[3]For examples of this second approach, see the following statements: *The Development of Moral and Spiritual Ideals in the Public Schools* (New York: Board of Education of the City of New York, 1956), p. 4; "Development of Moral and Spiritual Values through the Curriculum of California High Schools," *Bulletin of the California State Department of Education* XXI, No. 3 (September, 1952); National Education Association, *Moral and Spiritual Values in the Public Schools* (Washington: Educational Policies Commission, 1951).

teria discipline, and success of athletic teams, as signs of achievement in moral education.

Each of these examples offers some information as to the nature of moral education, but in each case the information is incomplete. Moral education is related to rules, as the first example implies. It is related to attitudes, as emphasized by the second example. And it is related to behaviors, as suggested by the Kentucky Movement.[4] However, each of these practical educational programs or statements relates to *only part* of the nature of the moral situation. Even taken together, these three examples give an incomplete picture of tasks and objectives in moral education. Thus, the practice of moral education (as represented in various historical examples) can only be of partial help in the attempt to understand moral education.

We may take a different approach to the problem of clearly identifying the subject of moral education by looking at three phrases similar to the term "moral education" in form—"science education," "driver education," and "business education." In each of these three phases there is a constant ("education") modified by a variable ("science," "driver," "business"). That is, we have "education" for three different types of experiences or situations. In science education the student is being prepared for or confronted with the nature of the scientific situation or experience. In driver education he is being prepared for the experience of driving a car, and in business education he is being prepared for aspects of the world of business. The same formula may be applied to the term "moral education" and we may then say that in moral education the student is being prepared for and/or confronted with the situation called the "moral situation" or "moral experience." Just as science, driving, and business are the respective subjects of science education, driver education, and business education, so the "moral" (i.e., the moral situation) is the subject of moral education. Furthermore, one would be foolhardy indeed to talk about—let alone to engage in—science education, driver education, or business education, without knowledge of the respective situations which serve as the foci of these educational pro-

---

[4]See the following for descriptions of the Kentucky Movement: E. F. Hartford, *Moral Values in Education* (New York: Harper and Brothers, 1959); and William C. Bower, *Moral and Spiritual Values in Education* (Lexington: University of Kentucky Press, 1952).

cesses. Similar caution must be exercised in reference to moral education; namely, one cannot talk about moral education without talking about the moral situation. The moral situation, then, is the central subject of moral education, and the first step in understanding moral education is clarification of the nature of the moral situation.

It is secondary *at this point* to ask what behaviors *should be* performed or what attitudes *should be* held in specific moral situations. This question is an important aspect of the analysis of moral education and should not be discarded under the guise of philosophic neutrality. However, the question is premature before one has dealt with the clarification of the moral situation itself.

The Moral Situation

What is a person doing, facing, or undergoing, when confronting a moral situation? What does it look like, feel like, sound like?

As indicated by one of the examples of moral education cited above, a moral situation is, first of all, one in which a *person is behaving or considering alternative behaviors.* In the moral situation a person acts or takes the steps necessary to choosing certain actions. It is, therefore, not exclusively a situation of communication (as, for example, in the linguistic or symbolic realm), or of experimentation (as in the empirical realm), or of contemplation (as in the synoptic realm). It is, rather, a situation of human confrontation with prospective behaviors and the choosing of alternatives. This, of course, tells us little about what the moral situation *is,* although it is valuable in distinguishing the moral situation from certain other situations. Thus, by this first criterion, we may say that animals do not face moral situations since they are not humans confronting alternative behaviors. Reading a newspaper is essentially not a moral situation since the act itself is not one of weighing alternatives and choosing (it may, of course, lead to a moral situation or choice). However, by the criteria so far established, a chess game, or deciding between several restaurants, or choosing a pair of shoes, may logically be a moral situation, since each of these examples involves humans weighing or choosing alternatives. Clearly, we must seek other components which will more precisely delineate the moral situation.

A second aspect of the moral situation, also implied by one of the examples of moral education programs cited above, is the role of *moral rules* or *principles,* i.e., statements pertaining to how one should act or what one ought to do.[5]

To clarify our understanding of the nature of moral principles, we turn first to the work of R. M. Hare.[6]

The first important aspect of the moral principle, as delineated by Hare, is its great similarity to an imperative statement. That is, a moral principle is a statement which conveys some directive or prescriptive force (the moral principle and the imperative together comprise the grammatical genus, "prescriptive language"). For example, the statements "You ought to obey your elders" and "Love thy neighbor as thyself" imply, at least, some directive or imperative toward one's behavior. However, Hare adds an important refinement to this aspect of the moral principle. It is *not* a prescription (in the strongest sense) made by one agent or authority, intended to directly cause certain behaviors in another agent. Rather, the moral principle is a weaker form of prescriptive statement. It does not directly cause, necessitate, or command behaviors, but *suggests* or *proposes* behaviors. Thus, Hare contends, the moral principle is not a directive made by authority *x* to agent *y;* rather, it is an "internal" suggestion which the agent himself uses in determining his behavior. The moral principle guides an individual's behavior by serving as a proposal or suggestion which he (the individual) *chooses* to guide his behavior. In this sense, moral principles only assume an imperative tone *if the agent himself accepts them as directives for his own behavior.*[7]

Hare is not prepared to follow some proponents of noncognitivism in saying that moral statements are totally imperatives. Rather, he is seeking some sort of rapprochement between naturalist and emotivist or noncognitivist theories. Thus, an important second theme of Hare's analysis is the existence of a *descriptive* component in moral principles. The descriptive component is that aspect of a moral statement which

[5]We shall use the terms "moral rule" and "moral principle" together, although not synonymously. For an analysis of the distinction, see Marcus Singer, "Moral Rules and Principles," Chapter 9 of this volume.

[6]*The Language of Morals* (1964); *Freedom and Reason* (1965); and "Universalisability," *Proceedings of the Aristotelian Society,* Vol. 55, 1954-55.

[7]For emphasis of this point, see: Jonas Soltis, "Men, Machines, and Morality," above; R. S. Peters, *Ethics and Education;* Erik Erikson, *Insight and Responsibility* (New York: W. W. Norton and Company, 1964).

conveys information about a situation or which points to certain accepted facts. The moral principle, then, describes a situation or presents information relevant to that situation as well as suggesting a course of action for the particular situation.[8]

However, the criteria of prescriptivity and descriptivity alone are insufficient for delineating the moral principle. For example, the statement "You ought to eat at Joe's Restaurant on King George Avenue" contains a descriptive component, referring to the act of eating at a certain restaurant on a certain street, as well as a prescriptive component, suggesting a certain behavior in reference to the situation described. Yet we would not consider this statement a moral principle.

In order to delineate the moral principle more precisely, we must refer to a third criterion posited by Hare: *universalizability*. The moral principle is not a rule or standard peculiar or relevant to a single individual in a single situation. Rather, it is a prescription relevant to a class or group of situations to be faced by an individual or individuals. The moral principle prescribes certain behaviors or attitudes for *anyone* who confronts any situation or experience of a certain type.

Adding this third element still does not fully delineate the moral principle. The following two examples fulfill the criteria of prescriptivity, descriptivity, and universality, yet one could legitimately argue that they are not moral principles:

1. "Everyone ought to eat at Joe's Restaurant when traveling" or "Everyone ought to eat when traveling"
2. "Everyone ought to obey traffic laws"

A fourth criterion necessary to fully define the moral principle is the notion of a theory of justification.[9] It is not sufficient to say that a moral statement is a universal prescription for behavior without also citing the necessity of a *justification* for prescribing or choosing certain behaviors. In every moral statement there is a posited assumption about the nature of the "good" or the "right" which is the reference point for

[8]The notion of the dual meaning of moral terms upon which Hare's analysis is based, has been introduced and argued at length in contemporary ethical theory by Charles L. Stevenson, in *Ethics and Language* (New Haven: Yale University Press, 1965). For a discussion of some problems with the dual theory, see George Kerner, *The Revolution in Ethical Theory* (New York: Oxford University Press, 1966).

[9]For an analysis of the role of a theory of justification in reference to the moral principle and moral reasoning, see Toulmin, *The Place of Reason in Ethics*.

the prescribing or choosing of certain actions. This means, in effect, that the alternative moral principles a person confronts reflect alternative conceptions of the "good" or the "right." If we now subject to this expanded description the counter-examples above, it becomes clear why they usually would not be considered moral statements. The described and prescribed activity in the first example is eating, and the justification for this activity would generally be in terms of "health" or "enjoyment" rather than "goodness" or "rightness." Similarly, the justification for obeying traffic laws would usually be made in terms of "the law of the land," and not in terms of inherent "goodness" or "rightness." However, if one *were to justify* certain eating habits or the obeying of traffic laws in terms of their (moral) goodness or rightness, then one would be quite correct in claiming that these statements were—for him— moral principles.

Thus, we now have a picture of the moral situation as one in which an individual, operating with certain principles or rules, confronts (optional) behaviors. The notion of optional or potential behaviors is a key to the next major component of the moral situation: *choice* (frequently referred to as the component of freedom or autonomy).[10] The very term "moral situation" implies an act or decision freely and consciously chosen by an individual, and not one performed as a result of external pressures or compulsion. The heart of the moral dilemma and situation is, in fact, the confrontation and wrestling with alternative options. The schoolboy who is *forced* to cheat by a friend is regarded as less morally culpable (and even perhaps morally innocent) than the schoolboy who has a free option to cheat or not, since in the first case there is not a *free choice*. The fact that the moral situation is one of potential alternative necessitates the fact that choice is a central aspect of the moral situation.

The introduction of choice as a key component of the moral situation reveals two other factors directly related to moral choice and hence to the moral situation: *reasoning* and *feelings*. Choice in the moral situation is guided by the presentation and consideration of reasons for

---

[10]For discussions of the autonomy factor, see: R. S. Peters, *Ethics and Education;* R. S. Peters, "Reason and Habit: The Paradox of Moral Education," in W. R. Niblett, ed., *Moral Education in a Changing Society;* R. M. Hare, "Adolescents into Adults," in T. B. Hollins, ed., *Aims in Education: The Philosophic Approach* (Manchester: Manchester University Press, 1964).

accepting or rejecting various alternatives. Such choice is not at all justifiable in terms of whim or personal taste alone. Nor is reference to reasons in itself satisfactory. The reasons referred to must be relevant to the particular choice being made. John Wilson cites the example of a person playing chess who makes his moves intentionally and for reasons, but for reasons which are not at all directly related to the purpose of the game.[11] For example, a person may make his moves so as to preserve a certain geometric pattern on the board. That is certainly a "reason" but not one relevant to the objectives of the particular situation. Similarly, there is a popular party game in which the group's replies to an individual's questions depend not at all on the content of the question but solely on the last letter of the last word of the question: if the last letter is a vowel, the answer is "yes"; if it's a consonant, the answer is "no." This too is justification in terms of reasons; but the reasons are unrelated to the content of the situation. In moral reasoning the problem is not to find reasons to justify one's choosing alternative behaviors. If such were the task, tradition, authority, or punishment could be an acceptable reason. The task, rather, is to find reasons which are directly related to the particular moral alternatives being faced. This means that the task is to find reasons which can justify a certain choice in terms of its moral goodness or rightness. Such a task is the activity of moral reasoning or justification, as opposed to moral rationalization.

While moral reasoning is a central part of the moral situation, it is also clear that there are some less rational or nonrational factors operative in such a situation. A person brings to the moral situation certain attitudes or feelings, the situation itself stimulates certain emotions, and the person leaves the situation with certain reactions and dispositions. These attitudes, emotions, and dispositions are not always related to the logic of the situation itself, rather to a host of extra-logical factors. Thus, moral choice does not involve the presentation of reasons alone. It also includes a change in or effect on one's dispositions, so as to insure the *acting upon* certain choices. The moral choice includes a state of mind—a positive attitude to acting upon what seems reasonable. William Frankena has emphasized this aspect of the moral sphere by distinguishing between the task of getting a person *to know* what is

[11] John Wilson, Norman Williams, Barry Sugarman, *Introduction to Moral Education* (London: Penguin Books, 1967), pp. 56-57.

morally right, and getting him *to act upon* this knowledge.[12] Thus, while one may wish to minimize as much as possible extraneous emotive factors in the moral situation, it is impossible to omit the emotive component when attempting to present a complete picture of the nature of the moral situation.

Our picture of the moral situation is almost complete. At this point, it includes an individual confronting a certain situation in which he must choose freely between certain behaviors with reference to certain criteria which include moral principles, moral reasons, and moral feelings.

However, even this description neglects the very nature of the particular situation itself as an influencing factor on the moral choice. The particular context in which the situation takes place—including, for example, the time of day, the year, city, street, weather, family circumstances—is important in that it may have an influence on the moral decision reached. Even if the decision is ultimately freely chosen by the agent, certain purely external (and nonmoral) factors over which he may have no control may play a role. Job bemoans the day he was born and the very fact of birth, but the fact remains that he *was* born and he *did not* die at birth. He is confronted with certain realities external to his own doing but relevant to his particular moral situation. The context of the moral situation itself, then, is an influencing factor in the moral situation.

We now have a picture of the moral situation which seems to logically delineate its particular nature. It is a situation in which an individual must choose between alternative behaviors or actions. This choice is guided by moral principles (which are universal prescriptions for behavior, embodying some theory of justification) and by a process of weighing reasons for the alternative choices. There are two nonmoral (and sometimes nonrational) factors which affect this choice—feelings brought to and caused by the situation, and the particular context of the situation. The *names* and *number* of components need not be considered the binding factor in the delineation of the moral situation. The crucial factor is the total picture presented by the components, and not necessarily the specific terminology or topology through which they are presented. Such a total picture is basic and prior to any attempt to intelligibly discuss the subject of moral education.

[12]See his exposition in "Toward a Philosophy of Moral Education," in Chapter 13 of this volume.

Educational Implications

It is not possible here to spell out in much detail the implications of this analysis for moral education. Three comments must suffice at this point.

First, it should again be emphasized that too much discussion of moral education has taken place without reference to the nature of the moral situation.

Second, many programs of moral education have taken into account only certain aspects of the moral situation while neglecting others. For example, a moral education which is rule-focused—i.e., which is essentially aimed at the transmission of moral rules and principles—neglects the role of choice, reasoning, feeling, behavior, context, in the moral situation. A behavior-focused moral education, concerned essentially with the development of desired behaviors by students, also emphasizes one aspect of the moral situation—behavior—at the expense of others. We find the history of moral education replete with examples of well-intended but inadequately rooted programs of moral education.

The third comment (which needs greater elaboration) is that the components of the moral situation as described above may be seen as the content and subject-matter of moral education. That is, the moral situation is the subject of study in moral education. How one effects such a study is a complex but crucial matter. One clue to such a study may be found in recent curriculum theory and projects. Thinking in that area has emphasized the importance of a student's "doing" science, mathematics, history, in a sophisticated sense; otherwise he may be said *not* to be *fully* studying these subjects. We may consequently suggest the following: in order to adequately study or participate in moral education, the student must be doing *moral* thinking. He must be immersed in, guided through, and made cognizant of the moral situation and its components. In that sense, one aspect of moral education demands that a student be a moral philosopher. Such a demand is educationally different from the other basic demand of moral education: that he be a moral person.

PART TWO *Justification*

in Ethics

"Why *should* I do that?"

"But how do I *know* that is right?"

"Can you *prove* it?"

Questions of this sort are the concern not only of the elementary and secondary school teacher engaged in moral education, but also of the philosopher involved with the explication of moral issues. These questions all deal with what is perhaps the central issue of a moral life: the justification of moral judgements. Few people would disagree with the assumption that we ought to do what is good or right. The thorny problem of ethics, however, is: How do we know and prove what is good or right?

There are two basic yet paradoxical positions which play a central role in most attempts to develop a theory of moral justification. The first position rests on the notion of *ethical objectivity*, i.e., the claim that there is some objective criterion which may be referred to in order to validate moral decisions and which is independent of purely local and personal views of what is moral. It is often argued that if there is no ethical objectivity, then there can be no moral truth or existence; in which case we are either doomed to moral anarchy or the very term "moral life" is rendered meaningless. Accordingly, many efforts to develop a theory of moral justification include the attempt to preserve the notion of ethical objectivity. A second basic position vis-à-vis the moral life is that it is in some way different and distinct from the empirical realm and that moral judgements are therefore not amenable to scientific validation. In short, it is held that the world revealed by science cannot totally prove or explain moral decisions. Thus, on the one hand there is an attempt to argue for ethical objectivity, and on the other hand there is a rejection of the binding force of science, the paragon of objectivity, for the moral sphere. Much of moral philosophy may be seen as an attempt to decide between, or to make peace between, these two apparently paradoxical positions.

One simple solution to this problem claims that there is no paradox at all; it denies that the moral and the natural sphere are distinct and argues that the empirical realm is binding for the moral life. A second simple solution insists that there is no way *out* of the paradox: that the moral and the empirical *are* totally distinct realms, that the empirical is *the* paradigm of objectivity, and that there is therefore no ethical objectivity. Much ethical theory, however, represents the attempt to build a theory of moral justification affirming both of the initial contentions while avoiding these simplistic solutions.

Phenix's argument, in the first chapter of this section, starts from the rejection of the naturalistic conception of morality as an aspect of the natural sphere. However, Phenix is concerned with retaining the objectivity of the moral order. His solution is the religious answer, the positing of an objective, nonnatural, ideal moral order rooted in a God notion. According to such an argument, there is ethical objectivity, but its roots are in an ideal and Divine, rather than an empirical, natural order. The acceptance or rejection of such a moral stance is rooted in a crucial nonmoral and more basic philosophic problem, i.e., the existence or nonexistence of an ideal metaphysical sphere.[1]

Moore's position is similar to Phenix's in its rejection of the equation of the natural and moral spheres, and in its affirmation of ethical objectivity. (Moore is, probably, the most significant twentieth-century expositor of these two arguments.) The major difference between Moore and Phenix is in their explanation of the nature of the *source* of ethical objectivity. According to Moore, ethical objectivity is rooted not in a Divine domain of ideal order but in the intuitive sphere of human life.

[1]For an introduction to the many problems of this position, see R. Taylor, *Metaphysics* (Englewood Cliffs, N.J.: Prentice-Hall, 1963).

That is, "good" is a nonnatural, nonanalyzable, simple property of things —a property which just *is,* which is perceived intuitively. Thus, there is an objective criterion (albeit intuitive) for the justification of moral judgements and decisions, according to Moore. The strength of such an argument is that it preserves ethical objectivity yet rejects naturalism, thereby avoiding the problem of empirical (scientific) "proof" of the "Good." The weakness of the position is the nature of the mechanism postulated to preserve objectivity, i.e., "intuition." Once again, as in the religious claim, the acceptance or rejection of a theory of justification is ultimately rooted in a nonmoral philosophic problem: in this case the existence or nonexistence of Moorean "intuition."

Morgenbesser's article is an attack on all such attempts to postulate a transcendent moral sphere. According to Morgenbesser, all such attempts to create transpersonal mechanisms of objectivity (e.g., intuition or an ideal order) create unnecessary and nonexistent mechanisms or present inaccurate and simplistic pictures of the nature of reality. These arguments for moral objectivism, he says, do emphasize one crucial point (the distinction between the moral and the empirical spheres); but they err in attempting to create a speculative and metaphysical mechanism in order to retain ethical objectivity. Morgenbesser also rejects the idea that moral justification lies in the domain of science. But he argues that there is nevertheless such a thing as objectivity in ethics, and that it is explained by the very real and observable fact that similar people in similar situations hold similar moral views and attitudes. That is, the notion of consensus of individual reactions to certain situations is Morgenbesser's answer to this problem. Ethical objectivity, then, is not rooted in rules of science, in theology, or in intuition, but in the voluntary sharing of attitudes among like-minded people.

The great appeal of the argument is that it enables a notion of ethical objectivity without resort to naturalism, theology, or intuition. There are, however, uncomfortable problems with such an argument. If it assumes that all like-minded people confronting similar situations will react uniformly, then it is simply a reformulation of a naturalist claim. The argument that all people cannot *help but react* to the same situation in the same manner (assuming, of course, that all conditions are identical) essentially assumes that there are "natural laws" which explain or justify moral decisions. If Morgenbesser is concerned with saying far less than this and arguing simply that the consensus of reaction to moral situations is the criterion of ethical objectivity, then he establishes the doubtful criterion of "majority rule" as the source of moral objectivism. Surely this would make little sense in connection with civil rights decisions and legislation in America, and would make a mockery of all men who have stood for "right" and "justice" against a majority.

Sartre's theory of moral justification is the next logical step after Morgenbesser's position in that he rejects empirical fact, ideal or Divine order, objective intuition, and group consciousness as the criterion of justification in morality. In fact, he is essentially willing to give up the very feature which Phenix, Moore, and Morgenbesser have sought to preserve, namely the notion of ethical objectivity. According to Sartre the justification of an action is the fact of its being freely chosen and done. The product or outcome of such an action may, of course, be deemed "immoral" by society (i.e., Mersault's act of murder in *The Stranger*); however, the act is supremely "moral," regardless of its outcome, if it is an expression of the agent's own choice and effort. Such a position, then, might well be seen as a theory based on the rejection of both of our starting assumptions. However, this is not really the case, for even in the Sartrean position there is an (objective) principle by which an action is deemed "moral" or not. Thus, even this position is rooted in the search for some criterion—and hence some way of retaining the notion—of ethical objectivity.

There are three important implications, for moral education, to be drawn from the philosophical problem of moral justification. First, any program of moral education either consciously or unconsciously is rooted in some theory of justification; i.e., every program of moral education assumes some criterion whereby decisions and actions are deemed morally "good" or "right." It is therefore imperative to make both teacher and student aware of these underlying criteria. Second, it would be difficult to talk about moral education if there were not some notion of ethical objectivity; i.e., if moral decisions were not in some way justifiable, the most that one could talk about would be moral conditioning, training, or indoctrination. Third, moral educators should realize that the dominant form of moral justification central to their program will determine to a large extent the content, methods, and objectives they choose. To make consistent choices, therefore, it behooves the moral educator to make quite explicit the form of moral justification upon which the program is to be built.

IV

*Ethics and the Will of God**
PHILIP H. PHENIX

Partly in reaction against . . . religious authoritarianism and partly in accordance with general secularizing tendencies, concerted efforts have been made to establish an autonomous humanistic ethics independent of all theological considerations. Much ethical analysis has been devoted to demonstrating that moral conduct does not require belief in God and consequently that moral education does not afford opportunity for the worship of God.

For example, in hedonistic ethics pleasure constitutes the test of goodness. The best act is one that leads to the greatest pleasure. In the egoistic form one's own pleasure is the standard. In the utilitarian form the greatest pleasure for the greatest number is the highest good. A somewhat broader conception of the good is found in the interest theory of ethics, such as proposed by Ralph Barton Perry. According to this view, a good is defined simply as an object of interest, and since interest, like pleasure, is an empirical human reaction, moral judgments can be made entirely on the basis of natural facts. If one has enough knowledge of psychology and sociology, patterns of value can in principle be calculated scientifically, without reference to any supernatural factors or to any mysterious moral intuitions.

* Reprinted with permission of the publisher from *Education and the Worship of God,* by Philip H. Phenix (Philadelphia: The Westminster Press, 1966), pp. 116-127. Copyright © MCMLXVI, W. L. Jenkins.

Other thinkers attempt to ground ethics in a naturalistic theory of human nature. Erich Fromm, for example, believes that it is possible in scientific psychology to construct a concept of the healthy personality and to use this construct as the basis for humanistic ethics. Similarly, Abraham Maslow presents a picture of the "self-actualizing personality" that he regards as an empirically-based standard of what a person ought to be.

All attempts to establish ethics on purely empirical foundations exhibit a major logical flaw, namely, the confusion of normative and factual meanings. It has long been recognized in ethical theory that judgments about what is right to do and good to attain can never be logically derived from any judgments of fact. What *ought* to be is of a different logical type from what *is*. To prove this assertion it is only necessary to observe that it is always appropriate to ask about any existing state of affairs whether or not it ought to exist. If one could logically deduce an obligation from a fact, then it would be self-contradictory to ask whether that fact ought to be what it is.

Therefore, all vaunted empirical systems of ethics, which derive their norms from factual data, contain implicit and unacknowledged normative premises that really negate their claim to strictly empirical status. An interest theory of value is logically tenable only on the basis of the suppressed normative premise that interest is good and that the pursuit of interest is right. Likewise, an ethics based on the description of the healthy person is logically acceptable only if the normative elements implicit in the definition of "healthy" are recognized.

This theoretical problem of the logic of ethical judgments is of far-reaching importance for moral education and for the religious dimensions in moral instruction. At issue is the legitimacy of one of the most ancient, insistent, and influential kinds of human insight and one of the perennial sources for the guidance of human conduct. If values are derivative from facts, it is educationally significant only to impart knowledge of what is. Questions about goodness and obligation then have no independent meaning, but must be reduced to questions of fact. In consequence, the scientific aspects of education are made central, and moral considerations are subordinated or eliminated altogether. Concern for the development of conscience is replaced by emphasis on factual knowledge.

This devaluation of distinctively moral understanding, in direct opposition to all the great religious traditions of mankind, is most evident in certain ethical theories, such as the one developed by Charles Stevenson, in which it is argued that moral statements have no cognitive content at all, but that they are merely expressions of feeling, associated with the desire that other people should feel likewise. The logic of moral discourse, it is said, is only that of emotional expression and of persuasion or command directed at arousing similar emotions in other people.

Such noncognitivism wholly undermines moral concern in education. It leaves no basis for meaningful ethical discussion and no grounds for instruction about right and wrong. Moral education is reduced to influencing other people in order to secure a larger degree of social conformity. Such instruction is essentially manipulative and propagandist. It certainly cannot be associated with the worship of God.

Serious moral education presupposes a cognitivist ethics. If moral statements are to be meaningfully discussed and if decisions concerning right and wrong are to be made responsibly, judgments of truth and falsity must apply in the ethical sphere. Moral truth is not of the same logical type as scientific truth. The methods of discovering and testing moral knowledge are not those of sense observation and experiment, nor are the theoretical categories in ethics the same as those in the empirical disciplines. Nevertheless, it is of basic importance for the moral enterprise that ethical assertions in some sense be subject to judgments of truth and falsity. If moral education is to be anything more than arbitrary indoctrination, there must be some kind of objective justification for ethical beliefs.

At stake here is the reality of the ideal order. The noncognitivist reduces ideals to subjective feelings. He holds that ideals are simply human hopes or wishes that just *are* and that cannot be called right or wrong in any objective sense. The cognitivist, on the contrary, holds that there is an objective ideal order to which the moral conscience responds, just as the empirical intelligence responds to the objective order of the world of fact. The connection of this issue with belief in God is evident. Whatever else he is, God is the Holy One, whose Will constitutes the objective moral order. If God is, then the ideal order is a powerful reality with which human beings are confronted and of which they must take account in their decisions. If God is not, then the basis for the ideal order becomes problematical or disappears altogether, and the only truth in which one can find security is that of empirical fact.

The efforts now being made to ground ethics in an empirical

science of human nature are evidence of a struggle to affirm the objective reality of the moral order without affirming God. They show how deeply felt is the need for a sound rational basis for moral conduct. At the same time, it is assumed that such a basis can be found only in the domain of finite fact. Yet since morality by definition concerns not what is but what ought to be, its basis must be sought in the realm of ideality and not of descriptive fact.

The search for moral foundations in human nature, for example, can succeed only if normative or ideal concepts of man are admitted. For a truly humanistic ethics, it is necessary to have a vision of what a person ought to become, of what a perfect human being would be like, and of the attributes of a really good man. These norms can never be derived from observing actual people nor from any kind of clinical data concerning mental health.

*   *   *

The search for some objective natural basis for morality is prompted by the fact of continuing disagreement about ethical standards. Knowledge of right and wrong is of great moment in human affairs, and yet no one has discovered a way of reaching a universal and stable consensus in this domain. This lack of a secure method puts ethics in sharp contrast with science, the power and appeal of which are due in large measure to its methods of public verification. To a far greater extent than matters of fact, judgments of right and wrong remain in dispute. Lacking the security of potentially universal agreement, ethical beliefs suffer in force and attractiveness as compared with scientific beliefs. For the same reason, moral education does not enjoy the prestige accorded to scientific education, nor are there systematic methods of improving moral understanding such as are available in scientific inquiry.

By reflection on the fact of continuing ethical disagreement, some important religious insights may result. Why do people differ in moral judgments so persistently? . . .

*   *   *

The . . . most important reason for moral disagreement is found in the very nature of morality as it concerns free and responsible personal decision. Both elements in morality, i.e., freedom and responsibility, are sources of continuing moral conflicts.

With respect to freedom, morality has to do with what a person wills to do and to become. It is not concerned with impersonal and objective matters, but with personal subjectivity. In making moral choices, a person acts to determine who he will become. No one path of life is necessary or determined in advance. An act performed because of external compulsion is not a moral act. To a large extent a person is the outcome of the choices he has made. In this sense everyone is a self-made man. Every decision contributes to the creation of a person's character, that is, to the habitual modes of behavior that pertain particularly to him.

The fundamental reason for moral disagreements is that each person tends to use his moral perspective as a justification for being the person he is. Everyone wants to feel secure in being who he is. Since no one enjoys feeling guilty and in the wrong, people try to avoid the sense of unworthiness by making virtue out of what they have freely elected to become. Instead of accepting an independent moral order that stands in judgment on them, they interpret their own standard of conduct as if it were an objective moral order. By so doing, they justify and confirm their personal identity.

The theological term for this process of self-justification is sin. A person is a sinner insofar as he makes himself the standard by which meaning and value are measured. The doctrine of original sin in Christian theology points to the tendency which seems to inhere in all human beings, regardless of inherited or cultural differences, to be primarily concerned with one's own security and satisfactions. Though this tendency can be camouflaged and to some degree mitigated, it can never be eradicated, and its apparent elimination in one sphere of activity usually causes it to appear in other forms in other areas of behavior.

From this standpoint, the phenomenon of moral disagreement is mainly a consequence of human freedom coupled with the sinful tendency to justify oneself by twisting moral judgments so as to confirm each person in the choices that have made him the person he is. Hence, consideration of moral issues in the school, particularly when persistent conflicts in belief about right and wrong are frankly faced, may lead to a recognition of the reality and seriousness of human freedom and of human sinfulness and to a growing realization of one's need for forgiveness and for deliverance from self-preoccupation. Such understanding is an important preparation for the worship of God. The divine omnipresence is not to be recognized only positively in the varied manifestations of meaning, order, and creative power in language, science, and the arts, but also negatively and by contrast in the moral struggles of human beings beset by fears and anxieties concerning self-justification.

The second element in morality besides freedom, and correlative with it, is responsibility. Having made a free choice, one is accountable for his decision. He is under judgment as to whether or not he acted rightly. In this respect moral choices differ essentially from conventional decisions, concerning, for example, the rules of a game or the symbols in a language or a mathematical system. Choices of aesthetic subjects and ways of expression in the arts are also for the most part truly arbitrary. In these nonmoral choices freedom is nonresponsible. The person decides what he will do without any question about justification. He makes his choice and that is the end of the matter. No questions are pertinent as to whether or not he ought to have acted as he did. Moral decisions, on the contrary, are free but not arbitrary, since the person who makes them is accountable for his acts.

Moral arguments, whether with oneself or with others, presuppose responsibility. They are attempts to render a satisfactory accounting or justification for what people decide to do. These attempts are accompanied by tension and anxiety. Life would be easier and more pleasant if decisions did not entail moral judgment. In order to escape the pain, uncertainty, and conflict, both within and without, that goes with responsibility, ways are sought to negate responsibility altogether.

One escape route is to deny that moral choice is free. What a person does, so the argument goes, is determined by factors over which he has no control. What is called freedom is only an illusion caused by the disparity between knowledge of the past and knowledge of the future. Human behavior, it is said, is governed entirely by factors of heredity and environment that are given rather than chosen or created by the person himself. In principle, it is possible on the basis of these given factors to predict the choices that will be made in any situation. Hence, freedom does not exist, and no one can reasonably be held accountable for his actions.

Such an escape, while theoretically possible, contradicts certain of the most fundamental data of human experience. A person knows himself as a conscious, creative, initiating center, not as a series of states in a determinate causal chain. As an initiator, he knows that his future is not wholly contained in his past, but that he has the ability within limits to construct his future, and therefore that he is responsible for what he causes to occur. The reality of responsibility stems from this fact of personal creativity and the genuine novelty of events that occur through human causation. A person's life is to a large extent of his own making. It does not agree with the most elemental human understanding to hold otherwise, that is, to say that a person's life is not really his, but is due to causes other than himself.

The other way of trying to evade responsibility is to assert that moral choices are absolutely free, in the sense that the rules of a game or the colors of a painting are. But such complete autonomy, without accountability, is clearly inconsistent with the fact that moral decisions are concerned with the quality of relationships. Moral choices always entail judgments of right or wrong, of better or worse, because they are never matters of private whim or personal preference. Each such decision is an affair of conscience, which is the subjective focus of moral responsibility.

It is in the light of morality as free and responsible decision that its essentially religious quality can be understood. In his freedom a human being manifests his likeness to God, the creative ground of all beings. When a person initiates a chain of events, he is, like God, a determiner of existence. It follows that moral instruction is concerned with making good the claim of man to be made in the divine image.

Since in moral choice one is not only free but also responsible, he makes his decisions in view of personal relationships. In its very nature responsibility is personal. One cannot be responsible to an impersonal rule, law, or principle. Responsibility is the ability to respond. It has meaning only in the relation of person to person. To be responsible is to be faithful to another person with whom one lives in a covenant of mutuality.

At the same time, the demand that conscience makes is not felt simply as an individual command. It is regarded as universal in its claim. The moral demand is objective. An action is right, not just for one person in a given situation, but for anyone in the same situation. The moral order plays no favorites. Its judgments are impartial and without respect to persons.

This seemingly paradoxical character or moral conscience—that it is simultaneously personal and yet above personal considerations—

points to the essentially religious nature of the moral encounter. God alone unites the personal and the transpersonal. He is the universal Person, the one who is the omnipresent source of personal being. He alone can be related in a fully personal way to each person in each situation and in that relationship bring to bear the persuasion and judgment of his universal righteous will.

Thus, serious reflection on what is implicit in every moral act conceived as free and responsible decision leads to the affirmation of God, and the assumption of responsibility for the right is seen to be a willing response to the will of God.

*   *   *

In religious perspective, being true to oneself is part of being true to God. The divine source of all being is the ground and goal of one's personal existence, and the worship of God is inseparable from the search for the divine will with respect to the person one ought to become. In reality, then, whenever education is conducted with the objective of responsible self-realization, it is an activity of divine worship.

V

The Indefinability of 'Good'*
G. E. MOORE

1. It is very easy to point out some among our every-day judgments, with the truth of which Ethics is undoubtedly concerned. Whenever we say, 'So and so is a good man,' or 'That fellow is a villain'; whenever we ask, 'What ought I to do?' or 'Is it wrong for me to do like this?'; whenever we hazard such remarks as 'Temperance is a virtue and drunkenness a vice'—it is undoubtedly the business of Ethics to discuss such questions and such statements; to argue what is the true answer when we ask what it is right to do, and to give reasons for thinking that our statements about the character of persons or the morality of actions are true or false. In the vast majority of cases, where we make statements involving any of the terms 'virtue,' 'vice,' 'duty,' 'right,' 'ought,' 'good,' 'bad,' we are making ethical judgments; and if we wish to discuss their truth, we shall be discussing a point of Ethics.

So much as this is not disputed; but it falls very far short of defining the province of Ethics. That province may indeed be defined as the whole truth about that which is at the same time common to all such judgments and peculiar to them. But we have still to ask the question: What is it that is thus common and peculiar? And this is a question to which very different answers have been given by ethical philosophers

*Reprinted with permission of the publisher from *Principia Ethica*, by G. E. Moore (Cambridge: Cambridge University Press, 1922), pp. 1-10.

of acknowledged reputation, and none of them, perhaps, completely satisfactory.

2. If we take such examples as those given above, we shall not be far wrong in saying that they are all of them concerned with the question of 'conduct'—with the question, what, in the conduct of us, human beings, is good, and what is bad, what is right, and what is wrong. For when we say that a man is good, we commonly mean that he acts rightly; when we say that drunkenness is a vice, we commonly mean that to get drunk is a wrong or wicked action. And this discussion of human conduct is, in fact, that with which the name 'Ethics' is most intimately associated. It is so associated by derivation; and conduct is undoubtedly by far the commonest and most generally interesting object of ethical judgments.

Accordingly, we find that many ethical philosophers are disposed to accept as an adequate definition of 'Ethics' the statement that it deals with the question what is good or bad in human conduct. They hold that its enquiries are properly confined to 'conduct' or to 'practice'; they hold that the name 'practical philosophy' covers all the matter with which it has to do. Now, without discussing the proper meaning of the word (for verbal questions are properly left to the writers of dictionaries and other persons interested in literature; philosophy, as we shall see, has no concern with them), I may say that I intend to use 'Ethics' to cover more than this—a usage, for which there is, I think, quite sufficient authority. I am using it to cover an enquiry for which, at all events, there is no other word: the general enquiry into what is good.

Ethics is undoubtedly concerned with the question what good conduct is; but, being concerned with this, it obviously does not start at the beginning, unless it is prepared to tell us what is good as well as what is conduct. For 'good conduct' is a complex notion: all conduct is not good; for some is certainly bad and some may be indifferent. And on the other hand, other things, beside conduct, may be good; and if they are so, then, 'good' denotes some property, that is common to them and conduct; and if we examine good conduct alone of all good things, then we shall be in danger of mistaking for this property, some property which is not shared by those other things: and thus we shall have made a mistake about Ethics even in this limited sense; for we shall not know what good conduct really is. This is a mistake which many writers have actually made, from limiting their enquiry to conduct. And hence I shall try to avoid it by considering first what is good in general; hoping, that if we can arrive at any certainty about this, it will be much easier to settle the question of good conduct: for we all know pretty well what 'conduct' is. This, then, is our first question: What is good? and What is bad? and to the discussion of this question (or these questions) I give the name of Ethics, since that science must, at all events, include it.

3. But this is a question which may have many meanings. If, for example, each of us were to say 'I am doing good now' or 'I had a good dinner yesterday,' these statements would each of them be some sort of answer to our question, although perhaps a false one. So, too, when A asks B what school he ought to send his son to, B's answer will certainly be an ethical judgment. And similarly all distribution of praise or blame to any personage or thing that has existed, now exists, or will exist, does give some answer to the question 'What is good?' In all such cases some particular thing is judged to be good or bad: the question 'What?' is answered by 'This.' But this is not the sense in which a scientific Ethics asks the question. Not one, of all the many million answers of this kind, which must be true, can form a part of an ethical system; although that science must contain reasons and principles sufficient for deciding on the truth of all of them. There are far too many persons, things and events in the world, past, present, or to come, for a discussion of their individual merits to be embraced in any science. Ethics, therefore, does not deal at all with facts of this nature, facts that are unique, individual, absolutely particular; facts with which such studies as history, geography, astronomy, are compelled, in part at least, to deal. And, for this reason, it is not the business of the ethical philosopher to give personal advice or exhortation.

4. But there is another meaning which may be given to the question 'What is good?' 'Books are good' would be an answer to it, though an answer obviously false; for some books are very bad indeed. And ethical judgments of this kind do indeed belong to Ethics; though I shall not deal with many of them. Such is the judgment 'Pleasure is good'— a judgment, of which Ethics should discuss the truth, although it is not nearly as important as that other judgment, with which we shall be much occupied presently—'Pleasure *alone* is good.' It is judgments of this sort, which are made in such books on Ethics as contain a list of 'virtues'

—in Aristotle's 'Ethics' for example. But it is judgments of precisely the same kind, which form the substance of what is commonly supposed to be a study different from Ethics, and one much less respectable—the study of Casuistry. We may be told that Casuistry differs from Ethics, in that it is much more detailed and particular, Ethics much more general. But it is most important to notice that Casuistry does not deal with anything that is absolutely particular—particular in the only sense in which a perfectly precise line can be drawn between it and what is general. It is not particular in the sense just noticed, the sense in which this book is a particular book, and A's friend's advice particular advice. Casuistry may indeed be *more* particular and Ethics *more* general; but that means that they differ only in degree and not in kind. And this is universally true of 'particular' and 'general,' when used in this common, but inaccurate, sense. So far as Ethics allows itself to give lists of virtues or even to name constituents of the Ideal, it is indistinguishable from Casuistry. Both alike deal with what is general, in the sense in which physics and chemistry deal with what is general. Just as chemistry aims at discovering what are the properties of oxygen, *wherever it occurs,* and not only of this or that particular specimen of oxygen; so Casuistry aims at discovering what actions are good, *whenever they occur.* In this respect Ethics and Casuistry alike are to be classed with such sciences as physics, chemistry and physiology, in their absolute distinction from those of which history and geography are instances. And it is to be noted that, owing to their detailed nature, casuistical investigations are actually nearer to physics and to chemistry than are the investigations usually assigned to Ethics. For just as physics cannot rest content with the discovery that light is propagated by waves of ether, but must go on to discover the particular nature of the ether-waves corresponding to each several colour; so Casuistry, not content with the general law that charity is a virtue must attempt to discover the relative merits of every different form of charity. Casuistry forms, therefore, part of the ideal of ethical science: Ethics cannot be complete without it. The defects of Casuistry are not defects of principle; no objection can be taken to its aim and object. It has failed only because it is far too difficult a subject to be treated adequately in our present state of knowledge. The casuist has been unable to distinguish, in the cases which he treats, those elements upon which their value depends. Hence he often thinks two cases to be alike in respect of value, when in reality they are alike only in some other respect. It is to mistakes of this kind that the pernicious influence of such investigations has been due. For Casuistry is the goal of ethical investigation. It cannot be safely attempted at the beginning of our studies, but only at the end.

5. But our question 'What is good?' may have still another meaning. We may, in the third place, mean to ask, not what thing or things are good, but how 'good' is to be defined. This is an enquiry which belongs only to Ethics, not to Casuistry; and this is the enquiry which will occupy us first.

It is an enquiry to which most special attention should be directed; since this question, how 'good' is to be defined, is the most fundamental question in all Ethics. That which is meant by 'good' is, in fact, except its converse 'bad,' the *only* simple object of thought which is peculiar to Ethics. Its definition is, therefore, the most essential point in the definition of Ethics; and moreover a mistake with regard to in entails a far larger number of erroneous ethical judgments than any other. Unless this first question be fully understood, and its true answer clearly recognised, the rest of Ethics is as good as useless from the point of view of systematic knowledge. True ethical judgments, of the two kinds last dealt with, may indeed be made by those who do not know the answer to this question as well as by those who do; and it goes without saying that the two classes of people may lead equally good lives. But it is extremely unlikely that the *most general* ethical judgments will be equally valid, in the absence of a true answer to this question: I shall presently try to show that the gravest errors have been largely due to beliefs in a false answer. And, in any case, it is impossible that, till the answer to this question be known, any one should know *what is the evidence* for any ethical judgment whatsoever. But the main object of Ethics, as a systematic science, is to give correct *reasons* for thinking that this or that is good; and, unless this question be answered, such reasons cannot be given. Even, therefore, apart from the fact that a false answer leads to false conclusions, the present enquiry is a most necessary and important part of the science of Ethics.

6. What, then, is good? How is good to be defined? Now, it may be thought that this is a verbal question. A definition does indeed often mean the expressing of one word's meaning in other words. But this is not the sort of definition I am asking for. Such a definition can never be of ultimate importance in any study except lexicography. If I want-

ed that kind of definition I should have to consider in the first place how people generally used the word 'good'; but my business is not with its proper usage, as established by custom. I should, indeed, be foolish, if I tried to use it for something which it did not usually denote: if, for instance, I were to announce that, whenever I used the word 'good,' I must be understood to be thinking of that object which is usually denoted by the word 'table.' I shall, therefore, use the word in the sense in which I think it is ordinarily used; but at the same time I am not anxious to discuss whether I am right in thinking that it is so used. My business is solely with that object or idea, which I hold, rightly or wrongly, that the word is generally used to stand for. What I want to discover is the nature of that object or idea, and about this I am extremely anxious to arrive at an agreement.

But, if we understand the question in this sense, my answer to it may seem a very disappointing one. If I am asked 'What is good?' my answer is that good is good, and that is the end of the matter. Or if I am asked 'How is good to be defined?' my answer is that it cannot be defined, and that is all I have to say about it. But disappointing as these answers may appear, they are of the very last importance. To readers who are familiar with philosophic terminology, I can express their importance by saying that they amount to this: That propositions about the good are all of them synthetic and never analytic; and that is plainly no trivial matter. And the same thing may be expressed more popularly, by saying that, if I am right, then nobody can foist upon us such an axiom as that 'Pleasure is the only good' or that 'The good is the desired' on the pretence that this is 'the very meaning of the word.'

7. Let us, then, consider this position. My point is that 'good' is a simple notion, just as 'yellow' is a simple notion; that, just as you cannot, by any manner of means, explain to any one who does not already know it, what yellow is, so you cannot explain what good is. Definitions of this kind that I was asking for, definitions which describe the real nature of the object or notion denoted by a word, and which do not merely tell us what the word is used to mean, are only possible when the object or notion in question is something complex. You can give a definition of a horse, because a horse has many different properties and qualities, all of which you can enumerate. But when you have enumerated them all, when you have reduced a horse to his simplest terms, then you can no longer define those terms. They are simply something which

you think of or perceive, and to any one who cannot think of or perceive them, you can never, by any definition, make their nature known. It may perhaps be objected to this that we are able to describe to others, objects which they have never seen or thought of. We can, for instance, make a man understand what a chimaera is, although he has never heard of one or seen one. You can tell him that it is an animal with a lioness's head and body, with a goat's head growing from the middle of its back, and with a snake in place of a tail. But here the object which you are discribing is a complex object; it is entirely composed of parts, with which we are all perfectly familiar—a snake, a goat, a lioness; and we know, too, the manner in which those parts are to be put to-gether, because we know what is meant by the middle of a lioness's back, and where her tail is wont to grow. And so it is with all objects, not previously known, which we are able to define: they are all com-plex; all composed of parts, which may themselves, in the first instance, be capable of similar definition, but which must in the end be reducible to simplest parts, which can no longer be defined. But yellow and good, we say, are not complex: they are notions of that simple kind, out of which definitions are composed and with which the power of further defining ceases.

8. When we say, as Webster says, 'The definition of horse is "A hoofed quadruped of the genus Equus,"' we may, in fact, mean three different things. (1) We may mean merely: 'When I say "horse," you are to understand that I am talking about a hoofed quadruped of the genus Equus.' This might be called the arbitrary verbal definition: and I do not mean that good is indefinable in that sense. (2) We may mean, as Webster ought to mean: 'When most English people say "horse," they mean a hoofed quadruped of the genus Equus.' This may be called the verbal definition proper, and I do not say that good is indefinable in this sense either; for it is certainly possible to discover how people use a word: otherwise, we could never have known that 'good' may be translated by 'gut' in German and by 'bon' in French. But (3) we may, when we define horse, mean something much more important. We may mean that a certain object, which we all of us know, is composed in a certain manner: that it has four legs, a head, a heart, a liver, etc., etc., all of them arranged in definite relations to one another. It is in this sense that I deny good to be definable. I say that it is not composed of any parts, which we can substitute for it in

our minds when we are thinking of it. We might think just as clearly and correctly about a horse, if we thought of all its parts and their arrangement instead of thinking of the whole: we could, I say, think how a horse differed from a donkey just as well, just as truly, in this way, as now we do, only not so easily; but there is nothing whatsoever which we could so substitute for good; and that is what I mean, when I say that good is indefinable.

9. But I am afraid I have still not removed the chief difficulty which may prevent acceptance of the proposition that good is indefinable. I do not mean to say that *the* good, that which is good, is thus indefinable; if I did think so, I should not be writing on Ethics, for my main object is to help towards discovering that definition. It is just because I think there will be less risk of error in our search for a definition of 'the good,' that I am now insisting that *good* is indefinable. I must try to explain the difference between these two. I suppose it may be granted that 'good' is an adjective. Well 'the good,' 'that which is good,' must therefore be the substantive to which the adjective 'good' will apply: it must be the whole of that to which the adjective will apply, and the adjective must *always* truly apply to it. But if it is that to which the adjective will apply, it must be something different from that adjective itself; and the whole of that something different, whatever it is, will be our definition of *the* good.

Now it may be that this something will have other adjectives, beside 'good,' that will apply to it. It may be full of pleasure, for example; it may be intelligent: and if these two adjectives are really part of its definition, then it will certainly be true, that pleasure and intelligence are good. And many people appear to think that, if we say 'Pleasure and intelligence are good,' or if we say 'Only pleasure and intelligence are good,' we are defining 'good.' Well, I cannot deny that propositions of this nature may sometimes be called definitions; I do not know well enough how the word is generally used to decide upon this point. I only wish it to be understood that that is not what I mean when I say there is no possible definition of good, and that I shall not mean this if I use the word again. I do most fully believe that some true proposition of the form 'Intelligence is good and intelligence alone is good' can be found; if none could be found, our definition of *the* good would be impossible. As it is, I believe *the* good to be definable; and yet I still say that good itself is indefinable.

10. 'Good,' then, if we mean by it that quality which we assert to belong to a thing, when we say that the thing is good, is incapable of any definition, in the most important sense of that word. The most important sense of 'definition' is that in which a definition states what are the parts which invariably compose a certain whole; and in this sense 'good' has no definition because it is simple and has no parts. It is one of those innumerable objects of thought which are themselves incapable of definition, because they are the ultimate terms by reference to which whatever *is* capable of definition must be defined. That there must be an indefinite number of such terms is obvious, on reflection; since we cannot define anything except by an analysis, which, when carried as far as it will go, refers us to something, which is simply different from anything else, and which by that ultimate difference explains the peculiarity of the whole which we are defining: for every whole contains some parts which are common to other wholes also. There is, therefore, no intrinsic difficulty in the contention that 'good' denotes a simple and indefinable quality. There are many other instances of such qualities.

Consider yellow, for example. We may try to define it, by describing its physical equivalent; we may state what kind of light-vibrations must stimulate the normal eye in order that we may perceive it. But a moment's reflection is sufficient to shew that those light-vibrations are not themselves what we mean by yellow. *They* are not what we perceive. Indeed we should never have been able to discover their existence, unless we had first been struck by the patent difference of quality between the different colours. The most we can be entitled to say of those vibrations is that they are what corresponds in space to the yellow which we actually perceive.

Yet a mistake of this simple kind has commonly been made about 'good.' It may be true that all things which are good are *also* something else, just as it is true that all things which are yellow produce a certain kind of vibration in the light. And it is a fact, that Ethics aims at discovering what are those other properties belonging to all things which are good. But far too many philosophers have thought that when they named those other properties they were actually defining good; that these properties, in fact, were simply not 'other,' but absolutely and entirely the same with goodness. . . .

VI

*Approaches to Ethical Objectivity**
SIDNEY MORGENBESSER

The relevance of ethical considerations for educational practice is a matter of general agreement. But the scope and methodology of ethical judgment is a subject of considerable controversy, both popular and philosophical. One of the fundamental points at issue is the possibility of objectivity in ethical judgment. Is such judgment a mere matter of subjective taste, or is it grounded in some nonpersonal standards? Certain recent thinkers have urged that a theological base is necessary to ground ethical objectivity, while others have sought in the data of perceptual psychology a guarantee of such objectivity. The first and second sections of this paper are devoted, respectively, to a critical analysis of these two trends, while the last sets forth an alternative interpretation of ethical objectivity and applies it to some educational issues.

I

Recent theologians have criticized what they take to be the root error of current philosophy: the denial by philosophers that values are objective. The issue according to the theologians is not simply an intellectual one, and its consequences not simply academic. For according to them unless values are proven to be objective, educational theory is

*Reprinted with permission of author and publisher from *Educational Theory,* Vol. 7, No. 3 (July, 1957), pp. 180-186.

baseless, the central problems of modern man will be intensified, and the drifts towards fascism or communism or both will be accelerated. Since the problem for these men is an urgent one, their refusal to wait for technical philosophers to perform a *volte-face* is at least understandable and their own attempts to prove objectivity by grounding ethics in a theology are at least honorable. But though there can be little doubt of their honor and earnestness, there is much confusion about their claim and program.

* * *

. . . Success of the theological program depends upon presentation of a series of definitions of ethical phrases and words in terms of theological ones, for otherwise, as we have already hinted, no deduction of ethics from theology would be achieved. But no such definitions are offered by proponents of this program and no definition that has historically been offered even seems plausible. At best, therefore, the recent theologians have offered us a series of blank checks. Of course, we can interpret them as making the same charge against the naturalists. But unless they produce adequate definitions, the superiority of *their* program is at best a matter of faith.

Two other comments about their program, however, independent of its ultimate success or failure, seem apposite. In discussing the problem of grounding ethics in a theology, they support the notion that moral theory is best presented as analogous to a geometry with one or two ethical axioms being sufficient, given relevant definitions, to deduce all the moral judgments we make. It is upon this small set of axioms that they concentrate when they demand a grounding of ethics. But after the general failure of formalistic rationalism as a philosophy of science, and after the searching criticisms of formalism in ethics given by Dewey and Stevenson, we may be antecedently dubious of the search for such axioms.

Secondly, in light of their program, their comments on the values that men currently entertain are puzzling. These writers frequently insist that, since philosophers have failed to supply a basis for values, men are currently adrift and, in some appropriate sense, do not know how to value. But this thesis is coupled with another to the effect that men as men *must* value, and that it is as difficult to find a nonvaluing man as it is rare to find a Spartan philosopher. I do not claim that there is an outright contradiction here. Most likely these critics would offer a distinction between *valuing* and *really valuing,* and insist that while modern men, as all men, must value they don't *really* value. I shall not consider the sociological grounds for this judgment about that vague entity 'modern man.' I emphasize only that it is hard to see the grounds upon which a distinction between values and real values can be made, without at the same time allowing that *many values are not really objective and not grounded.* Once again the simplified theological search for the objectivity of values becomes confusing.

I hope it is clear that in criticizing the account offered by these men about the causes of contemporary unrest, and by taking issue with their simplified version of present day philosophy, I am not asserting that all goes well in current life and thought. The materials for a dirge about our lot are readily available and need not be marshalled here afresh. I trust that it is equally apparent that in questioning the thesis that ethics needs a theological underpinning, I am not denying that there are many relevant *causal* connections between moral and religious institutions—connections which make it impossible to assert honestly and unequivocally Voltaire's plaint that the church is the greatest enemy of progress. But the *causal* relevance of church life is not the basis upon which recent theologians stake their claim; and can therefore be bypassed.

II

Gestalt psychologists like Wertheimer, Köhler, and Asch have attempted to prove that ethics is objective. These men generally restrict their attention to certain qualities which they call either "value-qualities" or (following that felicitous suggestion of Santayana), "tertiary-qualities" of objects and events. Their proof of the objectivity of ethics rests almost exclusively on the observation that value-qualities are perceived as being, to use their language, *in* the object. The gestaltists observe, and claim that we all observe an object as, e.g. terrifying, threatening, charming, etc., just as we observe an object as colored, solid, or heavy. Their observation is certainly a pregnant one; from it an entire philosophy is developed.

The gestaltists' perceptual doctrine seems cogent enough, and there would be little point discussing it were it not for the consequences they draw. They insist, if I read them correctly, that once we notice that value qualities are really there, we need not be puzzled about the basis of ethics, nor concern ourselves with the problem of the truth or falsity of ethical sentences. For in the same manner in which sentences about colors and shapes are supported by observational reports, ethical sentences are supported by observational reports about the perception of value qualities. The gestaltists' thesis is beguilingly simple; unfortunately, it seems false.

* * *

... In the first place, a quality is perceived under certain conditions, and the peculiarly *ethical* problem of deciding *whether to be* under those conditions is bypassed if we are simply informed of the nature of the perceptual experience *once we are there*. Secondly, the gestaltists encounter a difficulty which is reminiscent of one encountered by intuitionist philosophers like Professors D. Ross and A. C. Ewing, whose position may be mentioned in passing. According to the latter, ethical sentences are cognitive, i.e. true or false, not because they are accurate or inaccurate reports of certain qualities which, so to speak, clothe objects, but rather because they are accurate or inaccurate reports of the intuition of certain nonnatural qualities, qualities which by their very nature cannot be sensually perceived. But very few other philosophers find themselves intuiting the qualities mentioned and named by these philosophers, and hence most refuse to base an ethic on such nonnatural grounds. Similarly, many people find themselves missing the value-qualities the gestalt psychologists discern with ease. The cakes noticed by Alice had written 'eat me' upon them; the urchins noticed by gestalt psychologists are gilded 'help me.' But most of us share neither the perceptions of Alice nor those of the gestaltists.

Though gestalt psychologists have therefore not aided us in our quest for an objective basis for ethics, they are among the very few social scientists who have clearly realized that some relatively innocuous generalizations about the influence of groups or the importance of psychological drives cannot be substituted for an analysis of the rational grounds (if any) upon which ethical judgments may be decided and accepted. The bulk of other social scientific writings is generally irrelevant to our interests, because of failure to appreciate just this point.

III

Thus far we have attended in the main to some analyses of the word 'objective' which emphasize primarily the content or subject-matter of ethical sentences. Similar usages of the word 'objective' are found when nonethical sentences are being considered. Thus, it is in accord with common usage to assert that scientific sentences, such as Newton's laws, are objective in the sense that they concern phenomena independent of the judger or of any human being. But there is a second sense of the word 'objective' to which we now turn. In this second usage a sentence is considered objective if it is supported by evidence gathered in certain standard ways, and is one which can be agreed to by almost anyone willing to review the evidence in appropriate manner. These standard conditions will vary from domain of inquiry to domain of inquiry and cannot be specified once and for all; neither can the domains in which sentences are used in an objective manner be specified once and for all.

Now consider the domain of ethics and notice the patent fact that there are differences in the care with which support is marshalled for ethical decisions, just as there are differences in the care with which we support scientific judgments. Some may rant and rave, and impose their beliefs either about matters of fact or morals; others may be ready to support their views about the nature of the world or the rightness of certain acts carefully, slowly, considering all the factors and evidence involved. It is this difference in the care with which we support our judgments which enables us to speak of objectivity, in an important sense, both in science and ethics.

No one doubts, upon reflection, that ethical sentences are used on occasion in a careful and considerate manner, but many fail to see any connection between such deliberation and ethical *objectivity*. And indeed there would not be one unless a sense for the phrase 'evidence for ethical sentences' can be stipulated. In view of what we have said in the previous sections, it seems that the evidence for ethical sentences does not and cannot consist of reports of the perception of natural or non-natural qualities, nor does the evidence consist of an attempted deduction from axiomatic theology or perceptual psychology. What, then, does it consist of?

Attend for a moment to the intent of a person who insists that certain things are right. What does he mean? It seems to me that the person is attempting simultaneously to affirm something about his own approvals, and also to claim that if the person addressed knew of certain factors or if he underwent certain experiences, he would agree with him in attitude. If that is really his claim, then the evidence for the ethical sentence would consist of the probable agreement of the person addressed—agreement subsequent to the interchange of ideas, views and experience. It is because of this claim that people are ready to argue for their ethical positions. It is because of this claim that most people do not think that they are merely saying something about their own likes or dislikes when they assert ethical sentences, nor believe that they are merely uttering disguised imperatives to the listener. The reference to *empirical* connections between approvals and experiences is what distinguishes ethics from propaganda and emotive expression.

This way of approaching ethical issues is, of course, the classic naturalistic one, supported *inter alia* by Aristotle, Spinoza, Mill, and Dewey. Now these men have often been misinterpreted as teaching that a person supports his ethical claim by insisting that his attitude is more in accord with the needs and dictates of human nature than alternative ones. But this way of construing the issue is perverse. Prior to discussion no one has proof that his views are more grounded in the nature of man than the views of those who disagree with him. After discussion, the person who has convinced his listeners may announce that because the experience of discussion has sufficed to bring about a convergence of approvals, his views are truer to human nature. But this assertion adds nothing at all to the evidence. It is useful merely for decorative purposes.

The essential point will become clearer if elaborated from the perspective of one who desires his attitudes to be shared by others. At any given time, we have attitudes which are not shared by many, but we find ourselves unaffected by our singularity. The responses of others do not affect us on these issues. But there are issues concerning which we want others to share our attitude, and if we think our attitude a correct and justified one, one that should be shared because it is right and not simply because it happens to be ours, we are likely to use moral language. At such moments we may find ourselves face to face with at least one of the following four situations.

(1) There is no one who disagrees with us, at least no one whom we address, and since no one demands justification, the question of justification is not a serious one. Thus no teacher feels called upon to justify his attitude that a student not be flogged for absenting himself because of illness, before an audience of psychiatrists.

(2) Some of our listeners disagree with us, but they can be shown that the disagreement is merely apparent; caused to reflect they notice that the attitudes they already have support our suggestion in unsuspected ways. Thus a teacher may suggest to his colleagues the introduction of course A as a substitute for course B. At first his colleagues fail to see the point, but when the teacher offers evidence that the new course will lead to greater self-knowledge and greater sensitivity than course B did, his associates agree.

(3) The current attitudes of those who disagree with us are really in sharp contrast with ours. If we claim that we are right, i.e. if we claim that they would agree with us if they knew of certain factors or underwent certain experiences then we may indicate these. If after being under those conditions, those who had disagreed with us change their attitude and agree with us, we have justified our claim. On occasion, the conditions are easily specified and may consist merely of adding to the knowledge of our friends; on occasion the conditions are so intricate that they may never be specifiable. Thus a teacher who believes that no student should ever be graded may find it next to impossible to think of relevant conditions, and hence next to impossible to justify the claim.

(4) We may meet people who are not at all prepared to listen, and will not undertake any examination of their position. With such people, the possibilities of ethical argument are precluded. We may if we meet them retire to our chambers and conjure up an imaginary listener and think that if we have convinced him then we have won our case. And though such listeners may occasionally be severe, for the most part they conveniently agree with their creators. Or we may slowly and painfully walk alone, and think of a new day and a new generation when our suggestions will be listened to and followed. But though such visions succor and support us, we know we have proved nothing. Or we may, if the agreement is crucial, forget about proof and objectivity, and adopt force or political action.

If this analysis of ethical objectivity has any claim to support, then the following consequences follow for educational theory. In the first place, as has already been indicated, it would be futile for educators to search for a series of ethical principles which are to be used once and for all as a base; and it would be a worse mistake to justify any ethical principle by an alleged deduction from a set of sentences borrowed either from psychology or theology, unless it could be exhibited that ethical sentences were equivalent to them. On many occasions, educators will, as is to be expected, use moral language and insist that certain acts are right and certain states of affairs good. If their intent is, as suggested above, to claim that others will voluntarily, upon free discussion, share their attitudes, they can rest content that with the sharing that results from give and take, they have justified their claim and hence their ethic.

Moreover, if the notion of ethical objectivity sponsored in the last section is tenable, then it lends support to some of the best insights of great educators. For it has been the intent of such educators to maximize the number of occasions upon which discussions of right and wrong can take place, and it has been their intent to inculcate such habits as tenacity, courage, perception, and understanding, that make such discussion possible and fruitful. They have been suggesting *the spread of attitudes that make possible the discussion of attitudes.* The justification of the inculcation of these higher order attitudes can be undertaken in the same way as the justification of any other attitude, i.e. by discussion and interchange of experience, not by a search for some nonhuman support nor by a search for esoteric qualities. It is of course a commonplace that all of life is an education, and that we cannot expect more from *formal* education than a preparation for education from life. Yet many forget these commonplace observations and insist that the schools and the teachers inculcate a complete ethic. But if all of life is an education, we will continually change our attitudes and beliefs, and if formal education can be no more than a preparation for education from life, we cannot expect more from schooling than an inculcation of the attitudes that make objective discussion of attitudes possible. We can learn in our schools *how to proceed* in our ethical discussions; we cannot be prepared once and for all to know what is right and wrong. That through discussions we attempt to prove and not impose our ethic, and that such attempt with its associated skills constitutes the basis of ethical objectivity and a major goal of education is the burden of this paper.

VII

*Existentialism and Ethics**

JEAN PAUL SARTRE

I should like on this occasion to defend existentialism against some charges which have been brought against it.

First, it has been charged with inviting people to remain in a kind of desperate quietism because, since no solutions are possible, we should have to consider action in this world as quite impossible. We should then end up in a philosophy of contemplation; and since contemplation is a luxury, we come in the end to a bourgeois philosophy. The communists in particular have made these charges.

On the other hand, we have been charged with dwelling on human degradation, with pointing up everywhere the sordid, shady, and slimy, and neglecting the gracious and beautiful, the bright side of human nature; for example . . . with forgetting the smile of the child. Both sides charge us with having ignored human solidarity, with considering man as an isolated being. The communists say that the main reason for this is that we take pure subjectivity, the *Cartesian I think,* as our starting point; in other words, the moment in which man becomes fully aware of what it means to him to be an isolated being; as a result, we are unable to return to a state of solidarity with the men who are not ourselves, a state which we can never reach in the *cogito.*

*Reprinted with permission of the publisher from *Existentialism,* by Jean Paul Sartre (New York: The Philosophical Library, 1947), pp. 11-61.

From the Christian standpoint, we are charged with denying the reality and seriousness of human undertakings, since, if we reject God's commandments and the eternal verities, there no longer remains anything but pure caprice, with everyone permitted to do as he pleases and incapable, from his own point of view, of condemning the points of view and acts of others.

I shall try today to answer these different charges. Many people are going to be surprised at what is said here about humanism. We shall try to see in what sense it is to be understood. In any case, what can be said from the very beginning is that by existentialism we mean a doctrine which makes human life possible and, in addition, declares that every truth and every action implies a human setting and a human subjectivity.

As is generally known, the basic charge against us in that we put the emphasis on the dark side of human life. . . .

*   *   *

. . . Can it be that what really scares [people] in the doctrine I shall try to present here is that it leaves to man a possibility of choice? To answer this question, we must re-examine it on a strictly philosophical plane. What is meant by the term *existentialism?*

Actually, it is the least scandalous, the most austere of doctrines. It is intended strictly for specialists and philosophers. Yet it can be defined easily. What complicates matters is that there are two kinds of existentialist; first, those who are Christian, among whom I would include Jaspers and Gabriel Marcel, both Catholic; and on the other hand the atheistic existentialists, among whom I class Heidegger, and then the French existentialists and myself. What they have in common is that they think existence precedes essence, or, if you prefer, that subjectivity must be the starting point.

Just what does that mean? Let us consider some object that is manufactured, for example, a book or a paper-cutter: here is an object which has been made by an artisan whose inspiration came from a concept. He referred to the concept of what a paper-cutter is and likewise to a known method of production, which is part of the concept, something which is, by and large, a routine. Thus, the paper-cutter is at once an object produced in a certain way and, on the other hand, one having a specific use; and one can not postulate a man who produces a paper-cutter but does not know what it is used for. Therefore, let us say that, for the paper-cutter, essence—that is, the ensemble of both the production routines and the properties which enable it to be both produced and defined—precedes existence. Thus, the presence of the paper-cutter or book in front of me is determined. Therefore, we have here a technical view of the world whereby it can be said that production precedes existence.

When we conceive God as the Creator, He is generally thought of as a superior sort of artisan. Whatever doctrine we may be considering, whether one like that of Descartes or that of Leibnitz, we always grant that will more or less follows understanding or, at the very least, accompanies it, and that when God creates He knows exactly what He is creating. Thus, the concept of man in the mind of God is comparable to the concept of paper-cutter in the mind of the manufacturer, and, following certain techniques and a conception, God produces man, just as the artisan, following a definition and a technique, makes a paper-cutter. Thus, the individual man is the realisation of a certain concept in the divine intelligence.

In the eighteenth century, the atheism of the *philosophes* discarded the idea of God, but not so much for the notion that essence precedes existence. To a certain extent, this idea is found everywhere; we find it in Diderot, in Voltaire, and even in Kant. Man has a human nature; this human nature, which is the concept of the human, is found in all men, which means that each man is a particular example of a concept, man. In Kant, the result of this universality is that the wildman, the natural man, as well as the bourgeois, are circumscribed by the same definition and have the same qualities. Thus, here too the essence of man precedes the historical existence that we find in nature.

Atheistic existentialism, which I represent, is more coherent. It states that if God does not exist, there is at least one being in whom existence precedes essence, a being who exists before he can be defined by any concept, and that this being is man, or, as Heidegger says, human reality. What is meant here by saying that existence precedes essence? It means that, first of all, man exists, turns up, appears on the scene, and, only afterwards, defines himself. If man, as the existentialist conceives him, is indefinable, it is because at first he is nothing. Only afterward will he be something, and he himself will have made what he will be. Thus, there is no human nature, since there is no God to conceive it. Not only is man what he conceives himself to be, but he is also only what he wills himself to be after this thrust toward existence.

Man is nothing else but what he makes of himself. Such is the first principle of existentialism. It is also what is called subjectivity, the name we are labeled with when charges are brought against us. But what do we mean by this, if not that man has a greater dignity than a stone or table? For we mean that man first exists, that is, that man first of all is the being who hurls himself toward a future and who is conscious of imagining himself as being in the future. Man is at the start a plan which is aware of itself, rather than a patch of moss, a piece of garbage, or a cauliflower; nothing exists prior to this plan; there is nothing in heaven; man will be what he will have planned to be. Not what he will want to be. Because by the word "will" we generally mean a conscious decision, which is subsequent to what we have already made of ourselves. I may want to belong to a political party, write a book, get married; but all that is only a manifestation of an earlier, more spontaneous choice that is called [an act of] "will." But if existence really does precede essence, man is responsible for what he is.

Thus, existentialism's first move is to make every man aware of what he is and to make the full responsibility of his existence rest on him. And when we say that a man is responsible for himself, we do not only mean that he is responsible for his own individuality, but that he is responsible for all men.

The word subjectivism has two meanings, and our opponents play on the two. Subjectivism means, on the one hand, that an individual chooses and makes himself; and, on the other, that it is impossible for man to transcend human subjectivity. The second of these is the essential meaning of existentialism. When we say that man chooses his own self, we mean that every one of us does likewise; but we also mean by that that in making this choice he also chooses all men. In fact, in creating the man that we want to be, there is not a single one of our acts which does not at the same time create an image of man as we think he ought to be. To choose to be this or that is to affirm at the same time the value of what we choose, because we can never choose evil. We always choose the good, and nothing can be good for us without being good for all.

If, on the other hand, existence precedes essence, and if we grant that we exist and fashion our image at one and the same time, the image is valid for everybody and for our whole age. Thus, our responsibility is much greater than we might have supposed, because it involves all mankind. If I am a workingman and choose to join a Christian trade-union rather than be a communist, and if by being a member I want to show that the best thing for man is resignation, that the kingdom of man is not of this world, I am not only involving my own case —I want to be resigned for everyone. As a result, my action has involved all humanity. To take a more individual matter, if I want to marry, to have children; even if this marriage depends solely on my own circumstances or passion or wish, I am involving all humanity in monogamy and not merely myself. Therefore, I am responsible for myself and for everyone else. I am creating a certain image of man of my own choosing. In choosing myself, I choose man.

This helps us understand what the actual content is of such rather grandiloquent words as anguish, forlornness, despair. As you will see, it's all quite simple.

First, what is meant by anguish? The existentialists say at once that man is anguish. What that means is this: the man who involves himself and who realizes that he is not only the person he chooses to be, but also a law-maker who is, at the same time, choosing all mankind as well as himself, can not help escape the feeling of his total and deep responsibility. Of course, there are many people who are not anxious; but we claim that they are hiding their anxiety, that they are fleeing from it. Certainly, many people believe that when they do something, they themselves are the only ones involved, and when someone says to them, "What if everyone acted that way?" they shrug their shoulders and answer, "Everyone doesn't act that way." But really, one should always ask himself, "What would happen if everybody looked at things that way?" There is no escaping this disturbing thought except by a kind of double-dealing. A man who lies and makes excuses for himself by saying "not everybody does that," is someone with an uneasy conscience, because the act of lying implies that a universal value is conferred upon the lie.

Anguish is evident even when it conceals itself. This is the anguish that Kierkegaard called the anguish of Abraham. You know the story: an angel has ordered Abraham to sacrifice his son; if it really were an angel who has come and said, "You are Abraham, you shall sacrifice your son," everything would be all right. But everyone might first wonder, "Is it really an angel, and am I really Abraham? What proof do I have?"

*　　*　　*

Now, I'm not being singled out as an Abraham, and yet at every moment I'm obliged to perform exemplary acts. For every man, everything happens as if all mankind had its eyes fixed on him and were guiding itself by what he does. And every man ought to say to himself, "Am I really the kind of man who has the right to act in such a way that humanity might guide itself by my actions?" And if he does not say that to himself, he is masking his anguish.

There is no question here of the kind of anguish which would lead to quietism, to inaction. It is a matter of a simple sort of anguish that anybody who has had responsibilities is familiar with. For example, when a military officer takes the responsibility for an attack and sends a certain number of men to death, he chooses to do so, and in the main he alone makes the choice. Doubtless, orders come from above, but they are too broad; he interprets them, and on this interpretation depend the lives of ten or fourteen or twenty men. In making a decision he can not help having a certain anguish. All leaders know this anguish. That doesn't keep them from acting; on the contrary, it is the very condition of their action. For it implies that they envisage a number of possibilities, and when they choose one, they realize that it has value only because it is chosen. We shall see that this kind of anguish, which is the kind that existentialism describes, is explained, in addition, by a direct responsibility to the other men whom it involves. It it not a curtain separating us from action, but is part of action itself.

When we speak of forlornness, a term Heidegger was fond of, we mean only that God does not exist and that we have to face all the consequences of this. The existentialist is strongly opposed to a certain kind of secular ethics which would like to abolish God with the least possible expense. . . .

*　　*　　*

The existentialist, on the contrary, thinks it very distressing that God does not exist, because all possibility of finding values in a heaven of ideas disappears along with Him; there can no longer be an *a priori*

Good, since there is no infinite and perfect consciousness to think it. Nowhere is it written that the Good exists, that we must be honest, that we must not lie; because the fact is we are on a plane where there are only men. Dostoievsky said, "If God didn't exist, everything would be possible." That is the very starting point of existentialism. Indeed, everything is permissible if God does not exist, and as a result man is forlorn, because neither within him nor without does he find anything to cling to. He can't start making excuses for himself.

If existence really does precede essence, there is no explaining things away by reference to a fixed and given human nature. In other words, there is no determinism, man is free, man is freedom. On the other hand, if God does not exist, we find no values or commands to turn to which legitimize our conduct. So, in the bright realm of values, we have no excuse behind us, nor justification before us. We are alone, with no excuses.

That is the idea I shall try to convey when I say that man is condemned to be free. Condemned, because he did not create himself, yet, in other respects is free; because, once thrown into the world, he is responsible for everything he does. The existentialist does not believe in the power of passion. He will never agree that a sweeping passion is a ravaging torrent which fatally leads a man to certain acts and is therefore an excuse. He thinks that man is responsible for his passion.

The existentialist does not think that man is going to help himself by finding in the world some omen by which to orient himself. Because he thinks that man will interpret the omen to suit himself. Therefore, he thinks that man, with no support and no aid, is condemned every moment to invent man. Ponge, in a very fine article, has said, "Man is the future of man." That's exactly it. But if it is taken to mean that this future is recorded in heaven, that God sees it, then it is false, because it would really no longer be a future. If it is taken to mean that, whatever a man may be, there is a future to be forged, a virgin future before him, then this remark is sound. But then we are forlorn.

To give you an example which will enable you to understand forlornness better, I shall cite the case of one of my students who came to see me under the following circumstances: his father was on bad terms with his mother, and, moreover, was inclined to be a collaborationist; his older brother had been killed in the German offensive of 1940, and the young man, with somewhat immature but generous feelings, wanted to avenge him. His mother lived alone with him, very much upset by the half-treason of her husband and the death of her older son; the boy was her only consolation.

The boy was faced with the choice of leaving for England and joining the Free French Forces—that is, leaving his mother behind—or remaining with his mother and helping her to carry on. He was fully aware that the woman lived only for him and that his going-off—and perhaps his death—would plunge her into despair. He was also aware that every act that he did for his mother's sake was a sure thing, in the sense that it was helping her to carry on, whereas every effort he made toward going off and fighting was an uncertain move which might run aground and prove completely useless; for example, on his way to England he might, while passing through Spain, be detained indefinitely in a Spanish camp; he might reach England or Algiers and be stuck in an office at a desk job. As a result, he was faced with two very different kinds of action: one, concrete, immediate, but concerning only one individual; the other concerned an incomparably vaster group, a national collectivity, but for that very reason was dubious, and might be interrupted en route. And, at the same time, he was wavering between two kinds of ethics. On the one hand, an ethics of sympathy, of personal devotion; on the other, a broader ethics, but one whose efficacy was more dubious. He had to choose between the two.

Who could help him choose? Christian doctrine? No. Christian doctrine says, "Be charitable, love your neighbor, take the more rugged path, etc., etc." But which is the more rugged path? Whom should he love as a brother? The fighting man or his mother? Which does the greater good, the vague act of fighting in a group, or the concrete one of helping a particular human being to go on living? Who can decide *a priori?* Nobody. No book of ethics can tell him. The Kantian ethics says, "Never treat any person as a means, but as an end." Very well, if I stay with my mother, I'll treat her as an end and not as a means; but by virtue of this very fact, I'm running the risk of treating the people around me who are fighting, as a means; and, conversely, if I go to join those who are fighting, I'll be treating them as an end, and, by doing that, I run the risk of treating my mother as a means.

If values are vague, and if they are always too broad for the concrete and specific case that we are considering, the only thing left for us is to trust our instincts. That's what this young man tried to do; and when I saw him, he said, "In the end, feeling is what counts. I ought to choose whichever pushes me in one direction. If I feel that I love my mother enough to sacrifice everything else for her—my desire for vengeance, for action, for adventure—then I'll stay with her. If, on the contrary, I feel that my love for my mother isn't enough, I'll leave."

But how is the value of a feeling determined? What gives his feeling for his mother value? Precisely the fact that he remained with her. I may say that I like so-and-so well enough to sacrifice a certain amount of money for him, but I may say so only if I've done it. I may say "I love my mother well enough to remain with her" if I have remained with her. The only way to determine the value of this affection is, precisely, to perform an act which confirms and defines it. But, since I require this affection to justify my act, I find myself caught in a vicious circle.

On the other hand, Gide has well said that a mock feeling and a true feeling are almost indistinguishable; to decide that I love my mother and will remain with her, or to remain with her by putting on an act, amount somewhat to the same thing. In other words, the feeling is formed by the acts one performs; so, I can not refer to it in order to act upon it. Which means that I can neither seek within myself the true condition which will impel me to act, nor apply to a system of ethics for concepts which will permit me to act. You will say, "At least, he did go to a teacher for advice." But if you seek advice from a priest, for example, you have chosen this priest; you already knew, more or less, just about what advice he was going to give you. In other words, choosing your adviser is involving yourself. The proof of this is that if you are a Christian, you will say, "Consult a priest." But some priests are collaborating, some are just marking time, some are resisting. Which to choose? If the young man chooses a priest who is resisting or collaborating, he has already decided on the kind of advice he's going to get. Therefore, in coming to see me he knew the answer I was going to give him, and I had only one answer to give: "You're free, choose, that is, invent." No general ethics can show you what is to be done; there are no omens in the world. The Catholics will reply, "But there are." Granted—but, in any case, I myself choose the meaning they have.

•   •   •

As for despair, the term has a very simple meaning. It means that we shall confine ourselves to reckoning only with what depends upon our will, or on the ensemble of probabilities which make our action possible. When we want something, we always have to reckon with probabilities. I may be counting on the arrival of a friend. The friend is coming by rail or street-car; this supposes that the train will arrive on schedule, or that the street-car will not jump the track. I am left in the realm of possibility; but possibilities are to be reckoned with only to the point where my action comports with the ensemble of these possibilities, and no further. The moment the possibilities I am considering are not rigorously involved by my action, I ought to disengage myself from them, because no God, no scheme, can adapt the world and its possibilities to my will. When Descartes said, "Conquer yourself rather than the world," he meant essentially the same thing.

*   *   *

Given that men are free and that tomorrow they will freely decide what man will be, I can not be sure that, after my death, fellow-fighters will carry on my work to bring it to its maximum perfection. Tomorrow, after my death, some men may decide to set up Fascism, and the others may be cowardly and muddled enough to let them do it. Fascism will then be the human reality, so much the worse for us.

Actually, things will be as man will have decided they are to be. Does that mean that I should abandon myself to quietism? No. First, I should involve myself; then, act on the old saw, "Nothing ventured, nothing gained." Nor does it mean that I shouldn't belong to a party, but rather that I shall have no illusions and shall do what I can. For example, suppose I ask myself, "Will socialization, as such, ever come about?" I know nothing about it. All I know is that I'm going to do everything in my power to bring it about. Beyond that, I can't count on anything. Quietism is the attitude of people who say, "Let others do what I can't do." The doctrine I am presenting is the very opposite of quietism, since it declares, "There is no reality except in action." Moreover, it goes further, since it adds, "Man is nothing else than his plan; he exists only to the extent that he fulfills himself; he is therefore nothing else than the ensemble of his acts, nothing else than his life."

According to this, we can understand why our doctrine horrifies certain people. Because often the only way they can bear their wretch-edness is to think, "Circumstances have been against me. What I've been and done doesn't show my true worth. To be sure, I've had no great love, no great friendship, but that's because I haven't met a man or woman who was worthy. The books I've written haven't been very good because I haven't had the proper leisure. I haven't had children to devote myself to because I didn't find a man with whom I could have spent my life. So there remains within me, unused and quite viable, a host of propensities, inclinations, possibilities, that one wouldn't guess from the mere series of things I've done."

Now, for the existentialist there is really no love other than one which manifests itself in a person's being in love. There is no genius other than one which is expressed in works of art; the genius of Proust is the sum of Proust's works; the genius of Racine is his series of trage-dies. Outside of that, there is nothing. Why say that Racine could have written another tragedy, when he didn't write it? A man is in-volved in life, leaves his impress on it, and outside of that there is noth-ing. To be sure, this may seem a harsh thought to someone whose life hasn't been a success. But, on the other hand, it prompts people to un-derstand that reality alone is what counts, that dreams, expectations, and hopes warrant no more than to define a man as a disappointed dream, as miscarried hopes, as vain expectations. In other words, to define him negatively and not positively. However, when we say, "You are nothing else than your life," that does not imply that the artist will be judged solely on the basis of his works of art; a thousand other things will contribute toward summing him up. What we mean is that a man is nothing else than a series of undertakings, that he is the sum, the or-ganization, the ensemble of the relationships which make up these un-dertakings.

When all is said and done, what we are accused of, at bottom, is not our pessimism, but an optimistic toughness. If people throw up to us our works of fiction in which we write about people who are soft, weak, cowardly, and sometimes even downright bad, it's not because these people are soft, weak, cowardly, or bad; because if we were to say, as Zola did, that they are that way because of heredity, the workings of environment, society, because of biological or psychological determin-ism, people would be reassured. They would say, "Well, that's what we're like, no one can do anything about it." But when the existentialist writes about a coward, he says that this coward is responsible for his cowardice. He's not like that because he has a cowardly heart or lung or brain; he's not like that on account of his physiological make-up; but he's like that because he has made himself a coward by his acts. There's no such thing as a cowardly constitution; there are nervous constitutions; there is poor blood, as the common people say, or strong constitutions. But the man whose blood is poor is not a coward on that account, for what makes cowardice is the act of renouncing or yielding. A constitution is not an act; the coward is defined on the basis of the acts he performs. People feel, in a vague sort of way, that this coward we're talking about is guilty of being a coward, and the thought frightens them. What people would like is that a coward or a hero be born that way.

*　　*　　*

Thus, I think we have answered a number of the charges concerning existentialism. You see that it can not be taken for a philosophy of quietism, since it defines man in terms of action; nor for a pessimistic description of man—there is no doctrine more optimistic, since man's destiny is within himself; nor for an attempt to discourage man from acting, since it tells him that the only hope is in his acting and that action is the only thing that enables a man to live. Consequently, we are dealing here with an ethics of action and involvement.

*　　*　　*

. . . [We] may say that there is a universality of man; but it is not given, it is perpetually being made. I build the universal in choosing myself; I build it in understanding the configuration of every other man, whatever age he might have lived in. This absoluteness of choice does not do away with the relativeness of each epoch. At heart, what existentialism shows is the connection between the absolute character of free involvement, by virtue of which every man realizes himself in realizing a type of mankind, an involvement always comprehensible in any age whatsoever and by any person whosoever, and the relativeness of the cultural ensemble which may result from such a choice; it must be stressed that the relativity of Cartesianism and the absolute character of Cartesian involvement go together. In this sense, you may, if you like, say that each of us performs an absolute act in breathing, eating,

sleeping, or behaving in any way whatever. There is no difference between being free, like a configuration, like an existence which chooses
its essence, and being absolute. There is no difference between being
an absolute temporarily localised, that is, localised in history, and being
universally comprehensible.

*   *   *

The same holds on the ethical plane. . . . We can not decide *a priori*
what there is to be done. I think that I pointed that out quite sufficiently
when I mentioned the case of the student who came to see me, and
who might have applied to all the ethical systems, Kantian or otherwise, without getting any sort of guidance. He was obliged to devise
his law himself. Never let it be said by us that this man—who, taking
affection, individual action, and kind-heartedness toward a specific person as his ethical first principle, chooses to remain with his mother, or
who, preferring to make a sacrifice, chooses to go to England—has
made an arbitrary choice. Man makes himself. He isn't ready-made
at the start. In choosing his ethics, he makes himself, and force of circumstances is such that he can not abstain from choosing one. We
define man only in relationship to involvement. It is therefore absurd
to charge us with arbitrariness of choice.

*   *   *

. . . When I declare that freedom in every concrete circumstance
can have no other aim than to want itself, if man has once become
aware that in his forlornness he imposes values, he can no longer want
but one thing, and that is freedom, as the basis of all values. That
doesn't mean that he wants it in the abstract. It means simply that the
ultimate meaning of the acts of honest men is the quest for freedom
as such. A man who belongs to a communist or revolutionary union
wants concrete goals; these goals imply an abstract desire for freedom;
but this freedom is wanted in something concrete. We want freedom
for freedom's sake and in every particular circumstance. And in wanting freedom we discover that it depends entirely on the freedom of
others, and that the freedom of others depends on ours. Of course,
freedom as the definition of man does not depend on others, but as
soon as there is involvement, I am obliged to want others to have freedom at the same time that I want my own freedom. I can take freedom

as my goal only if I take that of others as a goal as well. Consequently, when, in all honesty, I've recognized that man is a being in whom existence precedes essence, that he is a free being who, in various circumstances, can want only his freedom, I have at the same time recognized that I can want only the freedom of others.

Therefore, in the name of this will for freedom, which freedom itself implies, I may pass judgment on those who seek to hide from themselves the complete arbitrariness and the complete freedom of their existence. Those who hide their complete freedom from themselves out of a spirit of seriousness or by means of deterministic excuses, I shall call cowards; those who try to show that their existence was necessary, when it is the very contingency of man's appearance on earth, I shall call stinkers. But cowards or stinkers can be judged only from a strictly unbiased point of view.

Therefore though the content of ethics is variable, a certain form of it is universal. Kant says that freedom desires both itself and the freedom of others. Granted. But he believes that the formal and the universal are enough to constitute an ethics. We, on the other hand, think that principles which are too abstract run aground in trying to decide action. Once again, take the case of the student. In the name of what great moral maxim do you think he could have decided, in perfect peace of mind, to abandon his mother or to stay with her? There is no way of judging. The content is always concrete and thereby unforeseeable; there is always the element of invention. The one thing that counts is knowing whether the inventing that has been done, has been done in the name of freedom.

PART THREE *Moral Principles*

The conventional approach to moral education assumes that the moral principle is at the heart of moral existence and that, consequently, the task of moral education is the transmission and inculcation of such principles. It is clear that moral life is in some direct sense linked to principles; it is less than clear, however, what is the nature and function of such principles. And it is even less clear, given the general dispersion of the idea of "relativity in ethics," that there are or can be any universally binding moral principles.

According to one important basic position, already noted, moral principles are definitive and determinant dictates for human behaviors, rooted in some absolute ground such as Divine will, Reason, or Society. Moral education according to such a conception would be as described above: the transmission and inculcation of these definitive principles. There are, however, several problems with such a conception. First, there is the essential question as to whether there do exist in fact any such absolute and determinant sources as God, Reason, or Society. Second, even if such sources exist, there is still reluctance to regard moral man as a person who simply acts in accord with imposed principles. Finally, one of the peculiarities of the moral life is that it is, in one important sense, meaningless to talk about the absoluteness or validity of moral principles for a person who does not accept them. That is, moral principles have absolutely no force or validity unless an agent has agreed to accept them and hence bind himself to their dictates. Thus, the validity of moral principles is in some sense conditional on their acceptance by the moral agent. In short, then, we see that the standard notion of moral principles as dictates is much less adequate than is normally assumed.

One key to clarification of the nature of moral principles is the distinction between the *content* of specific moral principles and the *function* of moral principles generally in moral deliberation and decision-making. In the content sense, moral principles do refer to a corpus of statements about desirable or correct behavior; e.g., "Love thy neighbor as thyself," "Honesty is the best policy," "Honor your elders." Such statements may be reflective of religious traditions, cultural values, or social norms, and they often are regarded as definitive directives for human behavior. Moreover, such emphasis on the content of the moral principle does imply a notion of moral education as concerned with the transmission and inculcation of a corpus of approved principles.

Most discussions of morality and moral education have been concerned with the content of specific moral principles. Much less attention has been paid to the *formal* aspect of the moral principle, i.e., to the *nature* and *function* of principles in moral life and education. Marcus Singer's analysis of moral rules and principles is concerned with such issues. In the first instance, Singer argues that there is a difference between "moral rules" and "moral principles," the former being guides to judgement which state that certain kinds of actions are generally right or wrong, while the latter state that certain kinds of actions are always right or wrong.[1] Moral rules then are more specific guides and indicators which are ultimately rooted in and derived from universalizable moral principles. On the basis of this distinction Singer goes on to discuss and question some of the claims of the theory of ethical relativism. His claim is that the so-called diversity of moral practices in different societies is more likely reflective of different moral *rules* (one of whose defining characteristics is their locality) rather than of different moral *principles*. Singer's ultimate argument is that there indeed are diverse

---

[1]For a different distinction between "moral rules" and "moral principles," in terms of threats versus ideals (or negative and positive directives), see E. Erikson, *Insight and Responsibility* (New York: W. W. Norton and Company, 1964), p. 222.

systems of moral rules, but these diverse systems can be traced to certain universalizable moral principles which are at the core of all moral life. The universalizable principles (the heart of which is the generalization principle) ultimately determine the frame and nature of specific codes of moral rules, rather than themselves constituting local substantive directives.

R. M. Hare is even more concerned than Singer with finding purely formal criteria for moral principles.[2] Hare's contention is that the moral principle is a prescriptive statement which guides moral decision-making. It is, thus, neither a definitive directive for moral behavior nor a descriptive statement of empirical fact. Rather, the moral principle contains both a descriptive element which indicates alternative moral options and a prescriptive element which suggests one of the alternatives. In addition, such statements do not refer to specific or local situations, but they come to prescribe behaviors for general categories of situations. Thus, moral principles are generalizable value statements which express alternative moral options to which the individual refers when confronting a moral decision.

On the basis of this notion of the moral principle, Hare speaks of the moral life as a life of "decisions of principle." It is the *reference to* and *decision on the basis of* principles, rather than casual or arbitrary choice, and rather than acceptance of principles *per se,* which defines the nature of moral existence. This in turn implies a notion of moral education as education for the principled life—education as transmission of the *principle of* CHOOSING AND ACTING ON MORAL PRINCIPLES. That is, moral education is concerned with inculcating not just specific moral rules or principles but, more important, the nature and role of principles in the moral sphere. Now one of the ways in which one learns how to choose and act on moral principles in general is obviously by learning specific rules and principles. However, the latter activity in itself cannot be regarded as exhausting moral education; it is, at the most, but one aspect, denotable as "moral training."

Different conceptions of the nature and function of moral principles will have important implications for alternative programs of moral education. While all systems may agree that principles are essential to the moral life, there will be profound differences between the

[2]See *The Language of Morals* (1964) and *Freedom and Reason* (1965).

contents, origins, and consequent pedagogy of moral principles in different systems. This means that the development of moral education programs must be rooted in and reflective of fundamental assumptions and commitments of moral philosophy such as those dealt with in this section.

VIII

Decisions of Principle*
R. M. HARE

... The question 'How shall I bring up my children?' which we
have mentioned, is one to the logic of which, since ancient times, few
philosophers have given much attention. A child's moral upbringing
has an effect upon him which will remain largely untouched by anything that happens to him thereafter. If he has had a stable upbringing, whether on good principles or on bad ones, it will be extremely
difficult for him to abandon those principles in later life—difficult but
not impossible. They will have for him the force of an objective moral
law; and his behaviour will seem to give much evidence in support of
intuitionist ethical theories, provided that it is not compared with the
behaviour of those who stick just as firmly to quite different principles.
But nevertheless, unless our education has been so thorough as to trans-
form us into automata, we can come to doubt or even reject these principles; that is what makes human beings, whose moral systems change,
different from ants, whose 'moral system' does not. Therefore, even if for
me the question 'What shall I do in such and such a situation?' is almost invariably answered without ambiguity by the moral intuition
which my upbringing has given me, I may, if I ask myself 'How shall I
bring up my children?' pause before giving an answer. It is here that

*Reprinted with permission of the author and publisher from *The Language
of Morals*, by R. M. Hare (Oxford: The Clarendon Press, 1964), pp. 74-78.

the most fundamental moral decisions of all arise; and it is here, if only moral philosophers would pay attention to them, that the most characteristic uses of moral words are to be found. Shall I bring up my children *exactly* as I was brought up, so that they have the same intuitions about morals as I have? Or have circumstances altered, so that the moral character of the father will not provide a suitable equipment for the children? Perhaps I shall try to bring them up like their father, and shall fail; perhaps their new environment will be too strong for me, and they will come to repudiate my principles. Or I may have become so bewildered by the strange new world that, although I still act from force of habit on the principles that I have learnt, I simply do not know what principles to impart to my children, if, indeed, one in my condition can impart any settled principles at all. On all these questions, I have to make up my mind; only the most hide-bound father will try to bring up his children, without thinking, in exactly the way that he himself was brought up; and even he will usually fail disastrously.

Many of the dark places of ethics become clearer when we consider this dilemma in which parents are liable to find themselves. We have already noticed that, although principles have in the end to rest upon decisions of principle, decisions as such cannot be taught; only principles can be taught. It is the powerlessness of the parent to make for his son those many decisions of principle which the son during his future career will make, that gives moral language its characteristic shape. The only instrument which the parent possesses is moral education—the teaching of principles by example and precept, backed up by chastisement and other more up-to-date psychological methods. Shall he use these means, and to what extent? Certain generations of parents have had no doubts about this question. They have used them to the full; and the result has been to turn their children into good intuitionists, able to cling to the rails, but bad at steering round corners. At other times parents—and who shall blame them?—suffer from lack of confidence; they are not sure enough what they themselves think, to be ready to impart to their children a stable way of life. The children of such a generation are likely to grow up opportunists, well able to make individual decisions, but without the settled body of principles which is the most priceless heritage that any generation can leave to its successors. For, though principles are in the end built upon decisions of principle, the building is the work of many generations, and the man who has to start from the beginning is to be pitied; he will not be likely, unless he is a genius, to achieve many conclusions of importance, any more than the average boy, turned loose without instruction upon a desert island, or even in a laboratory, would be likely to make any of the major scientific discoveries.

The dilemma between these two extreme courses in education is plainly a false one. Why it is a false one is apparent, if we recall what was said earlier about the dynamic relation between decisions and principles. It is very like learning to drive. It would be foolish, in teaching someone to drive, to try to inculcate into him such fixed and comprehensive principles that he would never have to make an independent decision. It would be equally foolish to go to the other extreme and leave it to him to find his own way of driving. What we do, if we are sensible, is to give him a solid basis of principles, but at the same time ample opportunity of making the decisions upon which these principles are based, and by which they are modified, improved, adapted to changed circumstances, or even abandoned if they become entirely unsuited to a new environment. To teach only the principles, without giving the opportunity of subjecting them to the learner's own decisions of principle, is like teaching science exclusively from textbooks without entering a laboratory. On the other hand, to abandon one's child or one's driving-pupil to his own self-expression is like putting a boy into a laboratory and saying 'Get on with it'. The boy may enjoy himself or kill himself, but will probably not learn much science.

The moral words, of which we may take 'ought' as an example, reflect in their logical behaviour this double nature of moral instruction—as well they may, for it is in moral instruction that they are most typically used. The sentences in which they appear are normally the expression of decisions of principle—and it is easy to let the decisions get separated, in our discussion of the subject, from the principles. This is the source of the controversy between the 'objectivists', as intuitionists sometimes call themselves, and the 'subjectivists', as they often call their opponents. The former lay stress on the fixed principles that are handed down by the father, the latter on the new decisions which have to be made by the son. The objectivist says 'Of course you know what you ought to do; look at what your conscience tells you, and if in doubt go by the consciences of the vast majority of men'. He is able to say this, because our consciences are the product of the principles which our early training has indelibly planted in us, and in one society these principles do not differ much from one person to another. The subjectivist, on the other hand, says 'But surely, when it comes to the point—when I have listened to what other people say, and given due weight to my own intuitions, the legacy of my upbringing—I have in the end to decide for myself what I ought to do. To deny this is to be a conventionalist; for both common moral notions and my own intuitions are the legacy of tradition, and—apart from the fact that there are so many different traditions in the world—traditions cannot be started without someone doing what I now feel called upon to do, decide. If I refuse to make my own decisions, I am, in merely copying my fathers, showing myself a lesser man than they; for whereas they must have initiated, I shall be merely accepting.' This plea of the subjectivist is quite justified. It is the plea of the adolescent who wants to be adult. To become morally adult is to reconcile these two apparently conflicting positions by learning to make decisions of principle; it is to learn to use 'ought'-sentences in the realization that they can only be verified by reference to a standard or set of principles which we have by our own decision accepted and made our own. This is what our present generation is so painfully trying to do.

IX

*Moral Rules and Principles**
MARCUS G. SINGER

It has generally been recognized that there is a distinction, of some importance, between moral rules and moral principles. Yet the distinction has not generally received explicit formulation, and there is no general agreement on just what it is. These terms tend to be used in different ways, and consequently the distinction between them has been drawn at different places. I shall make no attempt, however, to take account of all uses of these terms. Different purposes require different classifications and hence different distinctions. I shall use these terms in such a way that moral principles are more general, pervasive, and fundamental than moral rules, and in some sense their sources or grounds. It is in accordance with this usage that we sometimes speak of the principle underlying a certain rule, determining its scope and justifying exceptions to it. . . .

*　　　*　　　*

There are certain kinds of action or courses of conduct that are generally prudent or generally imprudent. It is, for example, generally imprudent to climb very high on a rickety ladder, especially if the

*Reprinted with permission of the publisher from *Essays in Moral Philosophy,* A. I. Melden, ed. (Seattle: University of Washington Press, 1958), pp. 160-197. Copyright © 1958, University of Washington Press.

rungs happen to be slippery. It follows that there are certain rules, called rules (or maxims) of prudence, to serve as guides to judgment, which state that certain kinds of actions are generally prudent or imprudent. Similarly, there are certain kinds of actions that are generally right or generally wrong, such as being kind to people, or depriving them of their rightful possessions. If an act is of a kind that is generally right or generally wrong, then it is governed by a moral rule. For a moral rule, as I shall understand the term, is simply a proposition to the effect that a certain kind of action is generally right or generally wrong. Any action of a kind that is generally wrong (or right) may reasonably be presumed to be wrong (or right), and, in the absence of any evidence to the contrary, is wrong (or right). Thus, while it is merely foolish to go against a rule of prudence without a good reason, it is immoral to violate or act contrary to a moral rule without a good reason. An act that violates a moral rule, or appears to do so, requires justification.

*   *   *

What I wish to emphasize here is that moral rules state what is right or wrong *usually*, or *for the most part*, though they may not be, and ordinarily are not, stated with this qualification. As examples of moral rules we may take the rules that stealing is wrong, that it is wrong to deceive people, and that everyone ought to keep his promises. The differences of verbal expression are irrelevant. These rules must all be understood with the qualification "generally," or "usually." It is not *always* wrong to lie; it is generally wrong. Similarly, it is not always right to keep a promise; it is generally right; and there are cases in which it is not only justifiable to break a promise, but wrong not to. To say that some kind of action is generally wrong is equivalent to saying that any action of that kind is wrong unless there is a reason to the contrary. (This obviously provides another way of defining moral rules.) To say that a certain kind of action is always wrong would be to say that an action of that kind would be wrong under any and all circumstances or conditions. And, as Mill has pointed out, "It is not the fault of any creed, but of the complicated nature of human affairs, that rules of conduct cannot be so framed as to require no exceptions, and that hardly any kind of action can safely be laid down as either always obligatory or always condemnable."[1] That moral rules require the qualification "generally" is shown by the fact of conflicting claims or obligations. Cases arise in which rules conflict; even if they did not arise in fact they could always be constructed.[2] An action of a kind that is generally wrong and also of a kind that is generally right would be a case of this sort (for actions can be described in different ways). Accordingly, under some circumstances it may be right, or even a duty, to break a promise, tell a lie, or take something that belongs to another without his permission.

* * *

So far I have been discussing moral rules, and have said little about how they differ from moral principles. A moral rule states that a certain kind of action is generally wrong (or obligatory), and leaves open the possibility that an act of that kind may be justifiable. Thus moral rules do not hold in all circumstances; they are not invariant; in a useful legal phrase, they are "defeasible." A moral principle, however, states that a certain kind of action (or, in some cases, a certain kind of rule) is always wrong (or obligatory), and does not leave open the possibility of justifying an action of that kind. Moral principles hold in all circumstances and allow of no exceptions; they are invariant with respect to every moral judgment and every moral situation. They are thus "indefeasible." It should be clear that such principles are bound to be somewhat more abstract than moral rules, though they are not necessarily less definite.

The principle of a rule can be thought of as analogous to the intent of a piece of legislation, which is the purpose it was designed to achieve, and hence the reason for its existence. Situations are constantly arising in which the literal or strict interpretation of a rule would be

[1] J. S. Mill, *Utilitarianism* (Everyman's Library ed.; New York: E. P. Dutton & Co., 1910), chap. ii, p. 23.

[2] One famous attempt to deny the possibility of a conflict of rules, or, to use the traditional terminology, a conflict of duties, was made by Kant. But in this case the denial is more aparent than real. For, though Kant denied the possibility of a conflict of duties, he did not deny, but rather affirmed, the possibility of conflicting *grounds of obligation*. See the Introduction to *The Metaphysic of Morals*, in T. K. Abbott (trans.), *Kant's Theory of Ethics* (6th ed.; London: Longman's, Green & Co., 1909), p. 280.

contrary to its intent or purpose. (This is the basis of the distinction between the spirit and the letter of the law.) In such situations the rule ought not to be applied. Thus, though one can have *some* understanding of a rule without understanding its intent, for an adequate understanding of the rule one should know the intent behind it. Only so can exceptions to it be made with justice and revisions of it be made with intelligence. (For a perfect understanding of a rule, one should, ideally, understand how it fits into the system of rules and the system of purposes they are designed to further.) Now a similar point applies to moral rules and principles. One can have some understanding of a moral rule without understanding how to apply moral principles. But for an adequate understanding of a rule one must know the principles on which it is based—to put it another way, the reasons on which it is established. This is one reason why reflection on morality is essential to morality.

Let us now consider some examples of moral principles. What I have called the generalization argument is one. The generalization principle is another. A third is the principle: "If the consequences of A's doing x would be undesirable, then A ought not to do x." Let us call this the *principle of consequences*. A fourth principle, obviously similar to the third, is: "It is always wrong to cause unnecessary suffering." A fifth principle concerns the character of moral rules and follows from what has already been said about them: "Any violation of a moral rule must be justified." This principle which is an obvious and immediate consequence of the generalization argument, may be called the *principle of justification*.

A little reflection suffices to show that it is impossible for any of these principles to conflict, though they are all closely related, and this is a further important difference between moral rules and principles.

*   *   *

There are at least three different kinds of moral rules which it is necessary to distinguish. Such rules as the ones against lying, killing, or stealing fall into a special class. These rules are fundamental moral rules. There are also what I propose to call "neutral norms," such as the rules of the road. Third, there are what might be called "local" rules. This class includes various standards, customs, and traditions, peculiar to different groups or communities, as well as such rules as the rule that everyone ought to pay his taxes. All these rules are similar in that a violation of them requires justification. But they are related in somewhat different ways to the generalization argument.

What I have called local rules are less comprehensive, and more closely tied down to their contexts and the purposes that justify them, than fundamental moral rules. Apart from being, as their name implies, more fundamental, the latter do not depend on variations in social or geographical conditions in the way local rules do, owing, perhaps, to their greater comprehensiveness (and generality) and relative freedom from context. It makes no sense to say of the rule to keep promises, for instance, that it may hold for one group of people and not for another. It does make sense to say this of the rule to pay taxes.

But let us consider first what I have called neutral norms. As an example of a neutral norm we may take the rule that everyone is required to drive on the right-hand side of the road. Such rules are *neutral* because it would make no moral difference if their opposites were adopted. This is the important difference between this type of rule and other rules. The rule just mentioned does not apply to people in England, where the rule is to drive on the left (and it might very well have been made a rule to proceed on red and stop on green). There is nothing antecedently (i.e., to the adoption of the rule) wrong about any of these activities. It is wrong (in the United States) to drive on the left-hand side of the road, as a consequence of the fact that the rule has been adopted and people are generally expected to obey it.

I have chosen the term "neutral norm" in analogy to Poincaré's term "neutral hypothesis." The characteristic of a neutral hypothesis is that "the same conclusions would have been reached by taking precisely the opposite," while it is necessary to make some assumption.[3] The characteristic of a neutral norm is that the same results would have been attained by adopting precisely the opposite, while it is necessary to adopt *some* rule.

That it is necessary to have some rule is established by the application of the generalization argument. What would happen if there were no rules for directing and ordering traffic, if everyone drove on the same side of the road, or on the side of the road on which he

[3]Henri Poincaré, "Science and Hypothesis," in *The Foundations of Science* (Lancaster, Pa.: Science Press, 1913), chap. ix, p. 135.

happened to feel like driving? There is no need to specify the details. It is surely clear that this would be, to say the least, extremely inconvenient, and this is sufficient to show that not everyone ought to drive on the same side of the road, and that no one has the right to drive on the side of the road on which he happens, at the moment, to feel like driving. It follows that everyone ought to drive on the right, or on the left—it does not matter which—in accordance with the rule of the community whose roads he is using, unless he has, as he might in special circumstances, good reason for the contrary. It obviously also follows that there must be some rule to prevent catastrophe and serve the needs roads were built to serve. It is clearly indifferent which rule is adopted, so long as it serves this purpose (and is not, on other grounds, obviously unjust or inconvenient).

It should be evident that a neutral norm involves an essential reference to a social need or purpose, which is advanced by the general observance of the rule and would be defeated by the general disregard of it. It is in terms of this need or purpose that it would be disastrous, or undesirable, if there were no such rule, and it is in terms of this need or purpose that the rule must be justified. Of course, a reference to expectations is also involved in the explanation of why it is wrong to disregard such a rule. People generally expect others to obey these rules and normally rely upon their doing so. But it is not wrong to violate such a rule *simply* because people expect and depend upon others to do so. This is no doubt part of the explanation. Yet, if no one obeyed such rules, probably no one would expect any one to do so. Hence the main reason it would be disastrous if no one obeyed such rules lies in the social needs such nonobservance would frustrate.

Now what I have called local rules also involve an essential reference to social needs and purposes, on which they depend and in terms of which they may be justified.

*   *   *

I have been arguing that moral principles are to be distinguished from moral rules by the fact that the former hold in all circumstances and do not admit of exceptions; that principles are invariant and do not vary with changes in circumstances or conditions; and that it is impossible for moral principles to conflict with one another. I have, furthermore, tried to show how moral principles—especially the two that I have called the generalization principle and the generalization argument—are involved in the establishment of moral rules, and how, in particular, they can establish different rules in different circumstances. In this connection, I distinguished between fundamental rules, local rules, and neutral norms. Local rules, I maintained, depend on local conditions in a way that fundamental rules do not, and hence are peculiar to, and differ with, different groups and communities—that is to say, different circumstances. Neutral norms are local rules that are conventional in a way that other rules are not, but both neutral norms and local rules depend on social needs or purposes that are advanced by their general observance and would be frustrated or defeated by their general violation. Hence changes in these needs or purposes would require changes in these rules.

I mention all this now not just to summarize the main features of an already complex argument, but to bring out the relevance of what I have been saying to the idea of cultural or moral relativity, and the closely associated theory of ethical relativism. By cultural relativity (or diversity) I understand the empirically ascertained fact that there are a great many different and even conflicting rules and practices prevailing at different times and in different places, so that (what at least appears to be) the same act may be regarded as right in one place and wrong in another. By ethical relativism I understand the theory that moral ideas are necessarily "relative to" a particular society, in the sense that they reflect the "standpoint" of some particular society and only "hold for" that society, so that in case of a conflict between these different standards there is no way of impartially or objectively deciding between them. Thus on this theory all moral judgments are incomplete unless they specify "the standpoint" from which they are made, and it is a further consequence of it that moral judgments are really expressions of the attitude or characteristics bias of a particular group. On this view, in other words, there is nothing that can correctly be said to *be* right or wrong, it is only a question of what is *called* "right" or "wrong," and by what group it is so called.

The fact of moral diversity, the fact that there are varities of moralities and moral codes, is of course a main source of the theory of ethical relativism. But it is not sufficient, by itself, to give rise to this theory. For this purpose other assumptions are required.

This theory arises, in the first place, from a failure to distinguish the invariant moral principles from the variable conditions that, in accordance with these principles, require or permit a variety of different rules and practices. Though practices and rules may be "relative," it does not follow that principles are. Yet this theory supposes that it does. It should really be obvious that moral principles, and I have in mind here especially the generalization principle and the generalization argument, do not require any uniformity of practices in different cultures. For they do not require any uniformity of practices in different circumstances. What is right in one context or set of circumstances may not be right in another, and differences in social or geographical conditions can count as relevant differences in circumstances. Thus what is right in Pomerania need not be right in Polynesia, or among the Dobuans, or in Rome. What is puzzling is that it should ever have been supposed that it should be so. For this general point, that moral principles are consistent with and allow for a wide variety of rules and practices, has often been made before (and from a variety of "standpoints"). . . .

*   *   *

. . . [In] the second place, this theory also arises out of the peculiar and question-begging assumption that if a certain practice prevails in a certain place then it is necessarily right in that place, that if a rule is not *recognized* by the members of a certain group then it does not *apply* to the members of that group. This assumption is not just peculiar; it is self-contradictory. One could, on this assumption, organize a group of thieves, who, by the mere fact that they like to steal, would be justified in stealing. On this view, one could justify himself in doing anything whatsoever merely by refusing to recognize any rule against it or by inculcating a taste for it. (For one person can constitute himself a society.) I have already pointed out how this is self-contradictory. If I were suddenly to hit you on the head with the jagged end of a broken bottle, for no reason at all, or "just because I felt like it," this would be immoral, and there is no possibility of justifying such an action (as distinct from getting away with it). For this is a case of wanton assault, of cruelty for the sake of cruelty, and this is always wrong, irrespective of circumstances. After the Indians in the Hudson Bay territory had obtained guns, it is reported, they "used to hunt Eskimos for sport, as we hunt bear or deer. . . . When eventually the Eski-

mos got guns, the Indians left them alone."[4] No doubt hunting Eskimos for sport was, at least for a time, part of the accepted practice of
this Indian community. But by no stretch of the imagination does it
follow that it was therefore justified, and I have already set forth the
principles on which this can be shown. It is one thing to record a practice, it is another to determine its moral standing.

[4]*New Yorker*, XXV, No. 17 (June 18, 1949), 30.

PART FOUR *Moral Sense*
and Autonomy

Much of the contemporary philosophy of moral education has been concerned with rejecting a conception of moral education as either "the transmission of moral principle" or "getting young people to act properly."[1] Instead, there has been a concentrated effort to argue for a conception of moral education which is rooted in the notion of moral thinking, understanding, and autonomy. According to such claims (key proponents: Dewey, Hare, Peters, Frankena, Wilson), the moral man is able to: (1) distinguish a moral from a nonmoral situation; (2) think intelligently about a moral situation and the various behavioral options in it; (3) choose a certain action on the basis of his considered evaluation; and (4) act accordingly.

Proponents of such a conception of moral education differ from radical progressive educators and from certain contemporary educational critics[2] in that the philosophers are not arguing for autonomy *per se* as the goal of moral education, but for autonomy within the context of

[1]For a developed example of critiques of the traditional position, see Wilson, Williams, and Sugarman, *Introduction to Moral Education,* Ch. 1.
[2]For a discussion of the new educational criticism, see S. McCracken, "Quackery in the Classroom," *Commentary,* Vol. 50, No. 2 (June, 1970).

disciplined moral thinking. Still, this "autonomy" conception is strikingly different from the aims of conventional contemporary programs of moral education (and indeed of many contemporary educational programs in general) in that it assumes that morality is as much an issue of thinking and choosing as it is of behaving. Consequently, much emphasis is placed on educating the student in the process of *thinking morally,* so that he will be prepared to make intelligent moral decisions rather than simply to *act* in moral ways. This means, of course, that the criteria for success of such a conception of moral education are rooted not in observable behaviors but in thought processes which lead up to such behaviors.

Hare's essay "Adolescents into Adults" is a clear exposition of such a position (it may also be seen as an educational expansion of philosophic assumptions presented in his "Decisions of Principle," Chapter 8). The specific subject of Hare's paper is the defining criterion of the concept "indoctrination."[3] In dealing with that issue, however, Hare develops a conception of moral education aimed at the preparation of students for autonomous moral decision-making. It is important to note that Hare presents a philosophic conception of the nature of moral *education* and not a psychological or sociological picture of the nature of moral *development.* His objective is to set the frame of the activity denoted as "moral education," *not* to present an empirical psychological description of moral development and *not* to propose an educational program for the practice of moral education. On the other hand, it is possible to argue that Hare himself ostensibly accepts the traditional psychological and pedagogic position that the child must be trained in certain behaviors until that time when he is able to "think about" moral issues. Hare claims, however, that there is a point when the child passes from "moral adolescence" into "moral adulthood." It is this *rite de passage* which must be the ultimate and central concern of the moral educator, even during the inescapable arbitrary and authoritarian periods of moral education.

John Wilson and the Farmington Trust Research Unit on Moral Education have been concerned with the notion of moral thinking and autonomy on two levels; on the philosophical level, in terms of the explication of the nature of morality, moral life, and moral education; and

---

[3]See also J. P. White, "Indoctrination," in R. S. Peters, ed., *The Concept of Education* (New York: The Humanities Press, 1967).

on the level of educational theory, in terms of the translation of theoretical assumptions into practical policy and programs.[4] Wilson and his colleagues have developed a comprehensive list of cognitive, affective, and behavioral components which, taken together, define the nature of "moral man" (and moral man so defined is popularly dubbed "the Farmington man"). These components in turn constitute the objectives and contents of moral education programs. The uniqueness of the Farmington man is not in his behaviors; it might be difficult to recognize or distinguish him on the street from the moral conformist or behaviorist. Rather, the Farmington man is distinguished by his motivations, thoughts and feelings, and by their influence on his behaviors. Such a conception of moral man and moral education obviously rules out an exclusively behavioral criterion of success and evaluation in moral education and instead implies the need for new forms of pedagogy and new evaluative procedures.

The third chapter in this section is written by a psychologist rather than a philosopher, although its assumptions and contents are remarkably congruent with the line of reasoning argued by Hare and Wilson. Kohlberg's psychological studies are rooted in the effort to elaborate a conception of "morality" in terms of a typology of general structures and forms of moral thought, rather than in terms of specific behaviors and actions. This typology encompasses three psychological levels, each containing two stages, and assumes a notion of morality as *procedure of moral thinking*. According to such a perspective, morality is developed and is evaluated in terms of moral thinking and the movement towards autonomous moral thinking, rather than in terms of a specific set of moral virtues or behaviors. Kohlberg's studies may be regarded as a valuable empirical continuation and elucidation of such philosophic conceptions as moral reasoning, thinking, and autonomy, which have been central themes of contemporary moral philosophy.

For the moral educator, the ideas discussed in these selections should make it clear that much thought needs to be given to the unique and specific forms of teaching and evaluation necessary to a form of moral education which emphasizes the autonomy of moral beings.

[4]The journal *Moral Education* is published in England by the Farmington Trust.

X

Adolescents into Adults*
R. M. HARE

. . . The two essential features of moral opinions are, first, that they
are not about matters of fact but about how one ought to behave (this
is what is meant by calling moral judgments 'prescriptive'); and secondly, that if I hold a certain moral opinion about an act done by one
person, I must hold the same moral opinion about a similar act done
by a similar person in similar circumstances. This is often referred to
by moral philosophers as the principle of the 'universalizability' of moral
judgments. Both of these are *logical* features of moral judgments; if we
do not understand either of them, we do not understand the uses of the
moral words. Roughly speaking, a moral opinion is *rational* if it is not
taken on authority as a matter of fact but freely accepted as a prescription for living, and if it is recognized as holding good irrespective of
whether it is I that am the subject of it or someone else. The reason
why, if someone transgresses either of these two requirements, he is not
being rational, is that they are requirements of logic, having their basis
in the meanings of the moral words; therefore someone who transgresses them is being as illogical as someone who says 'All the books
are red but there is one which is not.'

*Reprinted with permission of author and publisher from *Aims in Educa-
tion: The Philosophic Approach,* T. H. B. Hollins, ed. (Manchester: Manchester
University Press, 1964), pp. 59-70. © R. M. Hare.

Now the consequences of the first of these features of moral judgments for moral discussion have been adequately dealt with by Mr. Wilson.* Briefly, since moral judgments are not statements of fact or pieces of information, they cannot be taught out of a text-book like the names of the capitals of European countries. It is not a question of *informing* those whom we are teaching, but of their coming to accept a certain opinion for their own.

But Mr. Wilson did not, so far as I can remember, say anything about the second feature. Now, as I could show if I had time, it is this feature, in conjunction with the first, which really limits the moral opinions that we can hold. It is by applying these two characteristics of moral judgments together that argument really gets a grip on moral questions. What we have to teach people, if we are educating them morally, is to ask themselves the question 'What kind of behaviour am I ready to prescribe for myself, given that in prescribing it for myself, I am prescribing it also for anybody in a like situation?' I could, but I will not, go on to show how this question, if we can get people to ask it, circumscribes their moral choices in a rational way, so that the abandonment of taboos and irrational prejudices which Mr. Wilson recommends does not, as has sometimes been feared, open the way to unbridled license.

I said, 'If we can get people to ask it.' But one of the most important things for educators to remember is that morality, as governed by this question, is a very *difficult* thing to accept. Because it is a difficult and sophisticated thing, it does not come naturally to children. It is no use, as Mr. Wilson sometimes seems to imply, merely leaving children as free as possible from external moral influences, and hoping that the thing will just grow. It *will* grow in most cases, but only because the seed is there in our own way of thinking, from which it is well-nigh impossible to isolate a child. It is not, however, something innate; it is a question of tradition; morality is something that has to be handed down; if it were not—if the process were interrupted—our children really would grow up as barbarians.

What has to be passed on is not any *specific* moral principle, but

*Hare's references to "Mr. Wilson" in this essay refer to a lecture by John Wilson, also presented in *Aims in Education*. The reader should note that our next selection, by the same Mr. Wilson, is *not* the essay Mr. Hare is addressing himself to here.

an understanding of what morality is and a readiness to think in a moral way and act accordingly. This could be put in other words by saying that children have to learn to use the moral words such as 'right' and 'wrong' and to understand their meaning. That is why it is so very important for philosophers to study what their meaning is—how silly it is to say that philosophers ought not to occupy themselves with matters of words! It must be emphasized that it is not the content of any particular morality that is being handed down—that would be indoctrination, if the aim was, at all costs, to implant *these* particular moral principles. It is not a particular morality, but morality itself that we are teaching; not to think this or that (because we say so or because the good and great have said so) but to think morally for oneself. And to learn this is to learn how to *speak* morally, understanding what one says.

Doubtless it is not possible in practice to pass on the mere form of morality without embodying it in some content; we cannot teach children the abstract idea of a moral principle as such without teaching them some concrete moral principles. And naturally we shall choose for this purpose those principles which we think in themselves desirable. This, as I said, is not indoctrination provided that our aim is that the children should in the end come to appraise these princples for themselves. Just so, one cannot teach the scientific outlook without teaching some science; but the science that is taught could be radically altered in the light of later researches, and yet the scientific outlook remain. The good science teacher will teach what he thinks to be the truth, but his teaching will not have proved vain if what has been taught is later rejected as false; and similarly, if we can teach children what morality is, using our own moral thinking as an example, we shall have done our job, even if the moral thinking which they later do leads them to different conclusions.

Fortunately there is a close connexion between the form of morality and its content. As I could show if there were time, and have attempted to show in my book [*Freedom and Reason*], once the form of morality is accepted in our thinking, it quite narrowly circumscribes the substance of the moral principles that we shall adopt. We can therefore happily start by securing the adherence of our children—if necessary by non-rational methods—to the moral principles which we think best, provided that these are consistent with the form of morality; but we must leave them at liberty later to think out for themselves different principles, subject to the same proviso.

Now in conveying to children what morality is, our method is governed by what it is that we are trying to convey. Because moral judgments are things that one has to make for oneself, we have to get children to understand, in the end, that 'wrong' does *not* mean 'what the parent or the schoolmaster forbids'; the schoolmaster might forbid it, and the child might still think it right, and the child might have a right to its opinion. On this aspect of the matter Mr. Wilson has laid enough stress.

But secondly, and arising out of the universalizability of moral judgments, the child has got to realize, somehow, that what is wrong for another to do to him is wrong for him to do to another. This is the foundation of all that part of morality which concerns our dealings with other people. And this gives us an important clue about method. Children must learn to think about what it is like to be the other person. They must cultivate their sympathetic imaginations. And this is not easy. It will not be brought about without effort on the part of parents and schoolmasters. And it will not be brought about by rational discussion alone. Suppose that somebody who took Mr. Wilson too literally, and did not realize the importance of this feature of morality which he left out, went away from his lecture determined to confine himself, in his dealings with the young, in the early stages to plain imperatives like 'Go to bed', which make no pretence to be moral and therefore can do no harm, and in the later stages to rational discussion. His charges really would, if he could observe this principle in isolation from other influences, grow up without an understanding of morality.

Of course, this is unlikely to happen in practice, because there are, fortunately, other influences on children than their parents and schoolmasters, and many of them are media for the handing on of an understanding of moral thinking. The mere use of moral words by a child's contemporaries does a great deal. So nobody is going to be able to carry out this too literal interpretation of Mr. Wilson's prescription; and we are in no real danger of relapsing into a Hobbesian state of nature in which every man's hand is against every man. But unless *some* nonrational methods are used, it is unlikely that all our children will come to absorb this principle as deeply as we could wish; and to that extent less of their thinking about action will be moral thinking, and their actions will show this.

The non-rational influences I have in mind are chiefly two; environment, and example. The examples that one has set before one are *part* of one's environment, so this division is not a neat one; but it will do for what I want to say. The first important thing, if we want our children to learn morality, is that they should be put into an environment in which the unpleasant effects of other people's lapses on them are as obvious as possible. This means that they must have plenty of opportunity of rubbing up against other people in some sort of more or less constant group—more or less constant, because they have to have time to get to think of the other people in the group as people (i.e. as like themselves), or the treatment will not work. In such an environment, children can easily absorb the lesson that they ought to do unto others as they would that others should do unto them. The family is such a group; but families are not enough, because some families fall down on the job, and delinquency is sometimes the result. Schools, therefore, have a lot to contribute, as have clubs; and they have one very important advantage over the family, that in them the child rubs up against a large number of people of his own age, whom, therefore, it is easy for him to think of as like himself, sharing his likes and dislikes, and therefore hurt by the things that hurt him and pleased by the things that please him. It will be easier in such a group for the child to learn to universalize his moral judgments.

Secondly, the group must have a good tradition. If it is a St. Trinian's, the child will indeed suffer from the misdeeds of other children but its reaction will be one of self-defence merely, and we shall have a reign of blackboard jungle law. There has to be a tradition of kindness to, and co-operation with, other people. I am sorry to repeat these platitudes; but I want to show you how they are the consequences of the nature of morality; *that* they are true is obvious, but we need to understand *why* they are true.

But thirdly, how do we start these good traditions? This seems to me to be the most important, perhaps the only essential, function of the adult in moral education. After a certain age, children and young people will get their moral ideas and ideals and attitudes for the most part from each other; either from their schoolfellows or from the rest of the gang. So the most important point at which the adult can intervene, *if* he can intervene, is by influencing the morality of the group; and this is done by example.

Now I do not want you to make at this point what I think is a very easy mistake to make. 'Setting a good example' by itself is no use at all. The people to whom it is being set must want to follow it. We need to know what can make them want to follow it. I think that all good schoolmasters know the answer to this question. Children desire to imitate particular traits of a person whom they desire to imitate as a whole. If an adult is *merely* an example of desirable moral attitudes, they will not take much notice. But if there are a great many other things about him that they admire—usually things that have nothing to do with morals—then they will swallow the moral attitudes too.

There are a lot of things that children and young men will willingly learn from their elders. Sometimes, if they are intellectually gifted, they will even willingly learn from them Latin and French; but this is unfortunately not common. They will, however, very frequently be anxious to learn to play football, or sail boats, or play the violin in the orchestra; and if there is an adult whom they trust to teach them these things, they will pick up from him much besides. That is why those who are employing schoolmasters look, not merely for good teachers of Latin or French or football or music—they look for men who, in teaching these things, will hand on something that is of much more importance.

This is one of the sources of the value of so-called out-of-school activities like games and music, as well as the more wide-ranging ones like sailing and mountaineering, which are now becoming so popular. They are vehicles for the transmission of an understanding of morality from one generation to another. But they also have another importance from the moral point of view: all of them, to a greater or less extent, are co-operative activities; they therefore require, in all who participate in them, a standard of behaviour. On a small scale, but intensely, they reproduce those very factors which, I suppose, have led to the development of morality in civilized communities at large. One learns, in such teams or groups, to submit oneself to a rule—a rule not dictated by some particular person, but freely accepted by all the participants, either because, like the rule about not passing forward, or like watching the conductor, it is a necessary condition for the doing of *this* particular activity called orchestral playing or rugger; or else because it is dictated by the realities of the situation, like not sailing by the lee, or not getting lost in the mountains and causing other people to organize search parties to rescue you. The second of these two kinds of rules are the more important; and therefore I think that the second of the two kinds of activity—that which includes sailing and fell walking—deserves the increasing attention that it is getting from schoolmasters. Perhaps music should be after all included with these; for music also is in touch with reality; if you play a wrong note it is not just that you have broken the rule of a game. But games, in the narrow sense, will always have a certain artificiality. And of course compulsory games, whose rules are not freely accepted by the participants, do no good at all from the point of view that we are considering, though they may have some of the other virtues that used to be claimed for them.

The point that I wish to emphasize by saying these familiar things is that these practices, which schoolmasters have found useful, owe their usefulness to the nature of what they are trying to hand on, namely morality. Morality has, of its nature, to be freely accepted; therefore in this respect the rules of seamanship are a better analogue of it—and their strict observance actually a better example of it—than the rules in the school rule-book. And secondly, morality is impartial as between persons; therefore, to learn to accept rules applicable impartially within a group is a good schooling in morality. There is, of course, a danger in this; we all know the kind of team spirit which counts anything as fair against the other side, or against those outside the team. To become a loyal member of a group is an important step on the way from egoism to altruism; but it is a step at which it is all too easy to get stuck.

I must add here that, important as membership of groups is in the formation of moral ideas, it is important also for the development of the individual's personality that he should be able sometimes to break away from the group and pursue his own ideals, if necessary entirely by himself, if he is that sort of person. For all morality is not social morality—to think that it is, is a mistake that has often been made by moral philosophers and by educationists. There are moral ideals, some of them very fine ones, which have nothing to do with our fellow men; and although it is necessary to learn to live with our fellow men, it is restricting to the personality to be unable to get away from them. This educational requirement has, like the others, a theoretical basis in moral philosophy; but for reasons of time I shall not be able to tell you what it is.

I have mentioned two ways in which adults can help to pass on the idea of morality to another generation. But the power of adults to do this is severely limited by what adolescents will accept from adults. They want to imitate adults; but they want to imitate them in one thing above all—*in being adult.* They want, that is to say, to be their own masters. They will only feel that they have really succeeded in imitating the adult when they have got the adult out of the way.

This lends peculiar interest to an experiment which you may have seen described in *The Times* recently.[1] At Crawley, the local authority, having available some Nissen huts in a clearing in some woods near the town, turned them over without supervision to various youth organizations to use for a variety of purposes ranging from, I think, boxing to making model aeroplanes. The huts were intensively used, and looked after with very little damage, and obviously filled a need which must exist in other places than Crawley. When I say 'without supervision', this is not strictly accurate; there is a forest warden of the Forestry Commission who lives on the spot and keeps a fatherly eye on the buildings. But the point is that all the organization is done by the groups themselves without any adult interference. The success of this experiment should not make us ask, as apparently some people have asked, 'Are youth leaders (or for that matter schoolmasters) really necessary?' For of course good youth leaders and good schoolmasters will always be in short supply; what we learn from this experiment is one way of making the supply go further. Sometimes the best way adults can help adolescents to grow up is by keeping in the background; and of course this lesson has an application in schools too, and still more in universities.

It is by this readiness to retire gracefully, indeed, that we can most easily tell the educator from the indoctrinator. I said earlier that I agreed with Mr. Wilson that education might sometimes have to use the same methods as indoctrination, and that therefore the two cannot be distinguished by their methods. I said that they were distinguished by their aims; the educator is trying to turn children into adults; the indoctrinator is trying to make them into perpetual children. But I

[1]*The* [London] *Times,* Feb. 18, 1961, p. 9.

said that the aim would all the same make a difference to the method; and this becomes evident, if we watch the process over a period. Many of the methods I have alluded to can be used for indoctrination in the most deplorable doctrines; the Nazi youth organizations used them, fortunately without lasting success, to pervert a whole generation of German youth while they thought they were just youth-hostelling or playing games or whatever it might be. But if one watches carefully one will notice a difference. The educator is waiting and hoping all the time for those whom he is educating to start *thinking;* and none of the thoughts that may occur to them are labelled 'dangerous' *a priori.* The indoctrinator, on the other hand, is watching for signs of trouble, and ready to intervene to suppress it when it appears, however oblique and smooth his methods may be. The difference between these two is like the difference between the colonial administrator who knows, and is pleased, that he is working himself out of a job, and the one who is determined that the job shall still be there even when he himself retires.

So there is, in the end, a very great difference between the two methods. At the end of it all, the educator will insensibly stop being an educator, and find that he is talking to an equal, to an educated man like himself—a man who may disagree with everything he has ever said; and, unlike the indoctrinator, he will be pleased. So, when this happens, you can tell from the expression on his face which he is.

XI

Assessing the 'Morally Educated' Person*
JOHN WILSON

If the neutral and liberal picture of morality and moral education that
I have painted has to be accepted, we are committed to a programme
of research which might otherwise be very different. For instance, if
we defined a 'morally educated' person as somebody who did certain
easily-verifiable things (like giving money to charity), or held certain
easily-verifiable beliefs (such as that it was wrong to steal), we could
then proceed to discover the causes that produced 'morally educated'
people in this sense. Apart from the fact that any such definition would
be partisan, however, we have seen that even this would be less simple
than it sounds. For the concepts of action and belief are not so easily
turned into operational definitions. We would want to know, for instance, that a person was really doing something which we could rightly
and relevantly describe as 'giving his money to charity', as opposed, say,
to just avoiding super-tax or getting rid of a feeling of embarrassment
when he met with beggars: that he really believed that it was *wrong* to
steal, as opposed to believing (say) that it is nasty when his father
beats him for taking money from the till, or that it is bad to pinch from
one's friends but perfectly all right to diddle the income tax authorities.

*Reprinted with permission of the publisher from *Introduction to Moral
Education,* by John Wilson, Norman Williams, and Barry Sugarman (London:
Penguin Books Ltd., 1967), pp. 190-195. Copyright © The Farmington Trust,
1967.

In fact, however, the object of our concern is at once wider and more difficult to verify. It is wider, because what we want to know is the extent to which the moral thought and action of an individual is *rational* . . . or sane, and why it is: and it is more difficult to verify, because motives and intentions will play a far larger part in such verification than they would in any definition of 'moral education' which is tied down to particular beliefs and actions, difficult though they too might be.

We have in fact two tasks, which must be distinguished:

(i) Producing an operational definition of a 'morally educated' person; and

(ii) Discovering the preconditions and causal factors which produce such a person.

Both these tasks are enormous, but I want particularly to stress the first, which is apt to receive less than its fair share of attention. After what we have said earlier, we may now be conceptually clearer about what counts as a 'morally educated' person; but we are still a long way from being able to identify such a person in practice by means of tests, measurements, or any kind of verification-system. Yet until we can do this, our work on the preconditions and causal factors will be handicapped by our not being sure *what* it is we want to find the causes *of*. In other words, we want to be able to show that certain types of education produce 'morally educated' people: but unless we can first identify a 'morally educated' person, it will be hard to know what types of education to look for.

The general effect of what we have said . . . has perhaps been to enlarge our notion of moral education—to compel us to take into account various features which are essential to morality, and without which our picture of moral education would be dangerously one-sided. We can summarize the points very briefly as follows:

1. Overt behaviour by itself—'going through the motions'—is not sufficient for the notion of morality. A moral action is connected with intention and with acting for a reason: so that we have to know, not just what people do, but why they do it.

2. Only certain kinds of reasons will count as good reasons. We can't say 'Any reasons will do, so long as they lead to the right action': partly because we may have serious doubts about what in fact the 'right action' is, but chiefly because of the close connections between actions and reasons.

3. Good moral reasons must be based on a rational consideration of other people's interests: authority ('because so-and-so says so') or selfish desires ('because I feel like it') won't do by themselves.

4. A 'rational consideration' does not necessarily involve a great deal of conscious deliberation, but it involves such things as regarding other people as equals, knowing what their feelings are, respecting logic and the facts, not being deceived by linguistic confusion, and having moral rules or principles based on all these.

5. Finally, a man must have the ability to act on his moral principles: indeed, this would be one of the tests of whether he had really *committed* himself to the principles in the first place—whether they were really *moral* principles for him, as opposed to principles to which he paid only lip-service.

A List of Moral Components

What we need in order to make further progress is something like a phenomenological description of morality, which can be broken down into a number of components, each of which has some chance of being assessed in neutral terms. We have made some progress towards doing this, and the following scheme—though it is both vague and logically shaky—may be of interest. We have used the first few letters of a number of classical Greek words to give names to our components:

(a) PHIL refers to the degree to which one can identify with other people, in the sense of being such that other people's feelings and interests actually count or weigh with one, or are accepted as of equal validity to one's own. Different PHIL ratings might refer to the degree to which people are able to identify, and also to the range of this ability. Thus some people may identify very highly with, say, other gang-members, and not at all with old ladies: other people may identify very poorly with those of another class or colour, and so forth. (The degree with which one *ought* to identify in particular situations is of course in question here: but the general principle is that one ought to identify sufficiently to think and act in such a way as always to take their interests into account, regarding them as on an equality with oneself.) Like the other components, this is a matter of whether, in principle, one accepts others as equals: not a matter of how far one loves them, feels for them, etc.

(b) EMP refers to awareness or insight into one's own and other people's feelings: i.e., the ability to know what those feelings are and describe them correctly. A distinction might be drawn between self-awareness (AUTEMP) and awareness of others (ALLEMP). EMP does not of course logically imply PHIL, though as a matter of psychological fact it may be that one cannot develop in such a way as to have much EMP without also having PHIL. (Thus one can imagine a tyrant who, having EMP, could manipulate others cleverly, without regarding them as equals: but how many such cases exist in practice is a matter for further research.)

(c) GIG refers to the mastery of factual knowledge. To make correct moral decisions, PHIL and EMP are not sufficient: one also needs to have a reasonable idea of what consequences one's actions will have, and this is not entirely a matter of EMP. Thus a person might have enough EMP to know that negroes felt pain as much as white people did, and enough PHIL for this to count with him in making moral choices: but, through sheer ignorance rather than lack of EMP, believe that (say) because negroes have less nerve-endings or thicker skulls they do not get hurt so easily. Similarly Marie Antoinette ('let them eat cake') *may* have lacked GIG rather than EMP or PHIL.

(d) DIK refers to the rational formulation of EMP and GIG, on the basis of PHIL, into a set of rules or moral principles to which the individual commits himself, by the use of such universalizing words as 'good', 'right', etc., where these rules relate to other people's interests. There may be people, good at PHIL, EMP and GIG, who nevertheless do not pull all these together to make a set of consistent and action-guiding *principles,* or who draw their moral (or speudo-moral) principles irrationally from elsewhere.

(e) PHRON refers to the rational formulation of rules and principles (whether we call them moral or not) relating to one's own life and interests. Thus a drug addict or a suicide makes decisions which may affect virtually no one's interests but his own. There are, I think, reasons for saying that these choices are in some sense 'irrational', 'mentally unhealthy', or whatever. Such a person would be lacking in PHRON rather than in DIK. For PHRON, EMP (or at least AUTEMP) and GIG would be logically necessary. Whether PHIL is necessary—whether people can get to be aware of their own feelings, or even of factual consequences, without identifying with other people—is, as a *psychological* question, quite open. But logically they are distinct.

(f) KRAT refers to the ability to translate DIK or PHRON principles into action: to live up to one's moral or prudential principles. (One could distinguish between DIKRAT and PHRONKRAT if required. A person might be very conscientious towards other people but show a good deal of 'akrasia' or weakness of will about himself.) In talking of KRAT one is of course talking of the person who has genuinely decided on a principle, whether moral or prudential, but who is in some sense compelled to act otherwise: the model case is the addict.

Thus a typically 'morally educated' person would act as follows: he is driving a car, for instance. He identifies with other people sufficiently for their sufferings or inconvenience to count with him (PHIL). He knows how aggravating it is if a road-hog crowds one into the side of the road, or if one is held up by an unnecessarily slow driver (EMP). He knows that if, say, he drives his car at a steady 30 m.p.h. on a crowded main road, most people will want to pass him, because most cars cruise at more than 30 m.p.h. (GIG). Putting these together, he formulates and commits himself to a rule ('It is not right to drive at only 30 under these circumstances [sc. either for me or for anyone else]'), or ('One shouldn't crowd people into the side of the road') (DIK). He is then capable of acting on this principle, not carried away by fear of going too fast, or a desire to be obstructive or anything of that sort, and increases his speed (KRAT). Some average of these might perhaps be made to give a general 'moral education' rating (ARI).

Though this framework is certainly extremely crude, and may have important logical gaps, I quote it here chiefly in order to show the general direction of our thinking, which is (it seems to me) the direction that any such large-scale enquiry which is not based on partisan values must take. It should not be beyond our powers to devise some means of assessing the ratings of these various components. We should then be in a position to do a number of interesting things; for instance:

(i) One could detect just which components were missing in certain classes or groups of people e.g. delinquents, teenagers, etc., or particular sub-groups of these: and conversely with groups that might have a high ARI rating.

(ii) One could detect what measures increased what ratings (e.g. it is a reasonable guess that the use of films with discussions, etc. would increase EMP).

(iii) One could make a more intelligent guess about what sorts of things schools ought to try, once one knows more precisely where the weak components are.

It goes without saying that the general findings of psychology and sociology would give us at least a clear lead as to the causes of high or low ratings and there would be interesting comparisons with social class, I.Q. and many other things.

XII

*The Child as a Moral Philosopher**
LAWRENCE KOHLBERG

How can one study morality? Current trends in the fields of ethics, linguistics, anthropology and cognitive psychology have suggested a new approach which seems to avoid the morass of semantical confusions, value-bias and cultural relativity in which the psychoanalytic and semantic approaches to morality have foundered. New scholarship in all these fields is now focusing upon structures, forms and relationships that seem to be common to all societies and all languages rather than upon the features that make particular languages or cultures different.

For 12 years, my colleagues and I studied the same group of 75 boys, following their development at three-year intervals from early adolescence through young manhood. At the start of the study, the boys were aged 10 to 16. We have now followed them through to ages 22 to 28. In addition, I have explored moral development in other cultures—Great Britain, Canada, Taiwan, Mexico and Turkey.

Inspired by Jean Piaget's pioneering effort to apply a structural approach to moral development, I have gradually elaborated over the years of my study a typological scheme describing general structures and forms of moral thought which can be defined independently of the specific content of particular moral decisions or actions.

*Reprinted with permission of the publisher from *Psychology Today* Magazine, September 1968, pp. 25-30. Copyright © Communications/Research/ Machines, Inc.

The typology contains three distinct levels of moral thinking, and within each of these levels distinguishes two related stages. These levels and stages may be considered separate moral philosophies, distinct views of the socio-moral world.

We can speak of the child as having his own morality or series of moralities. Adults seldom listen to children's moralizing. If a child throws back a few adult cliches and behaves himself, most parents—and many anthropologists and psychologists as well—think that the child has adopted or internalized the appropriate parental standards.

Actually, as soon as we talk with children about morality, we find that they have many ways of making judgments which are not "internalized" from the outside, and which do not come in any direct and obvious way from parents, teachers or even peers.

Moral Levels

The *preconventional* level is the first of three levels of moral thinking; the second level is *conventional,* and the third *postconventional* or autonomous. While the preconventional child is often "well-behaved" and is responsive to cultural labels of good and bad, he interprets these labels in terms of their physical consequences (punishment, reward, exchange of favors) or in terms of the physical power of those who enunciate the rules and labels of good and bad.

This level is usually occupied by children aged four to 10, a fact long known to sensitive observers of children. The capacity of "properly behaved" children of this age to engage in cruel behavior when there are holes in the power structure is sometimes noted as tragic *(Lord of the Flies, High Wind in Jamaica),* sometimes as comic (Lucy in *Peanuts).*

The second or *conventional* level also can be described as conformist, but that is perhaps too smug a term. Maintaining the expectations and rules of the individual's family, group or nation is perceived as valuable in its own right. There is a concern not only with *conforming* to the individual's social order but in *maintaining,* supporting and justifying this order.

The *postconventional* level is characterized by a major thrust toward autonomous moral principles which have validity and application apart from authority of the groups or persons who hold them and apart from the individual's identification with those persons or groups.

Moral Stages

Within each of these three levels there are two discernible stages. At the preconventional level we have:

Stage 1: Orientation toward punishment and unquestioning deference to superior power. The physical consequences of action regardless of their human meaning or value determine its goodness or badness.

Stage 2: Right action consists of that which instrumentally satisfies one's own needs and occasionally the needs of others. Human relations are viewed in terms like those of the marketplace. Elements of fairness, of reciprocity and equal sharing are present, but they are always interpreted in a physical, pragmatic way. Reciprocity is a matter of "you scratch my back and I'll scratch yours" not of loyalty, gratitude or justice.

And at the conventional level we have:

Stage 3: Good-boy–good-girl orientation. Good behavior is that which pleases or helps others and is approved by them. There is much conformity to stereotypical images of what is majority or "natural" behavior. Behavior is often judged by intention—"he means well" becomes important for the first time, and is overused, as by Charlie Brown in *Peanuts*. One seeks approval by being "nice."

Stage 4: Orientation toward authority, fixed rules and the maintenance of the social order. Right behavior consists of doing one's duty, showing respect for authority and maintaining the given social order for its own sake. One earns respect by performing dutifully.

At the postconventional level, we have:

Stage 5: A social-contract orientation, generally with legalistic and utilitarian overtones. Right action tends to be defined in terms of general rights and in terms of standards which have been critically examined and agreed upon by the whole society. There is a clear awareness of the relativism of personal values and opinions and a corresponding emphasis upon procedural rules for reaching consensus. Aside from what is constitutionally and democratically agreed upon, right or wrong is a matter of personal "values" and "opinion." The result is an emphasis upon the "legal point of view," but with an emphasis upon the possibility of *changing* law in terms of rational considerations of social utility, rather than freezing it in the terms of Stage 4 "law and order." Outside the legal realm, free agreement and contract are the binding elements of obligation. This is the "official" morality of American government, and finds its ground in the thought of the writers of the Constitution.

Stage 6: Orientation toward the decisions of conscience and toward self-chosen *ethical principles* appealing to logical comprehensiveness, universality and consistency. These principles are abstract and ethical (the Golden Rule, the categorical imperative); they are not concrete moral rules like the Ten Commandments. Instead, they are universal principles of *justice,* of the *reciprocity* and *equality* of human rights, and of respect for the dignity of human beings as *individual persons.*

Up to Now

In the past, when psychologists tried to answer the question asked of Socrates by Meno "Is virtue something that can be taught (by rational discussion), or does it come by practice, or is it a natural inborn attitude?" their answers usually have been dictated, not by research findings on children's moral character, but by their general theoretical convictions.

Behavior theorists have said that virtue is behavior acquired according to their favorite general principles of learning. Freudians have claimed that virtue is superego-identification with parents generated by a proper balance of love and authority in family relations.

The American psychologists who have actually studied children's morality have tried to start with a set of labels—the "virtues" and "vices," the "traits" of good and bad character found in ordinary language. The earliest major psychological study of moral character, that of Hugh Hartshorne and Mark May in 1928-1930, focused on a bag of virtues including honesty, service (altruism or generosity), and self-control. To their dismay, they found that there were *no* character traits, psychological dispositions or entities which corresponded to words like honesty, service or self-control.

Regarding honesty, for instance, they found that almost everyone cheats some of the time, and that if a person cheats in one situation, it doesn't mean that he *will* or *won't* in another. In other words it is not an identifiable character trait, *dis*honesty, that makes a child cheat in a given situation. These early researchers also found that people who cheat express as much or even more moral disapproval of cheating as those who do not cheat.

What Hartshorne and May found out about their bag of virtues is equallly upsetting to the somewhat more psychological-sounding names introduced by psychoanalytic psychology: "superego strength," "resistence to temptation," "strength of conscience," and the like. When recent researchers attempt to measure such traits in individuals, they have been forced to use Hartshorne and May's old tests of honesty and self-control and they get exactly the same results—"superego strength" in one situation predicts little to "superego strength" in another. That is, virtue-words like honesty (or superego-strength) point to certain behaviors with approval, but give us no guide to understanding them.

So far as one can extract some generalized personality factor from children's performance on tests of honesty or resistance to temptation, it is a factor of ego-strength or ego-control, which always involves non-moral capacities like the capacity to maintain attention, intelligent-task performance, and the ability to delay response. "Ego-strength" (called "will" in earlier days) has something to do with moral action, but it does not take us to the core of morality or to the definition of virtue. Obviously enough, many of the greatest evil-doers in history have been men of strong wills, men strongly pursuing immoral goals.

Moral Reasons

In our research, we have found definite and universal levels of development in moral thought. In our study of 75 American boys from early adolescence on, these youths were presented with hypothetical moral dilemmas, all deliberately philosophical, some of them found in medieval works of casuistry.

On the basis of their reasoning about these dilemmas at a given age, each boy's stage of thought could be determined for each of 25 basic moral concepts or aspects. One such aspect, for instance, is "Motive Given for Rule Obedience or Moral Action." In this instance, the six stages look like this:

— 1. Obey rules to avoid punishment.
  2. Conform to obtain rewards, have favors returned, and so on.
  3. Conform to avoid disapproval, dislike by others.

4. Conform to avoid censure by legitimate authorities and resultant guilt.
5. Conform to maintain the respect of the impartial spectator judging in terms of community welfare.
6. Conform to avoid self-condemnation.

In another of these 25 moral aspects, the value of human life, the six stages can be defined thus:

1. The value of a human life is confused with the value of physical objects and is based on the social status or physical attributes of its possessor.
2. The value of a human life is seen as instrumental to the satisfaction of the needs of its possessor or of other persons.
3. The value of a human life is based on the empathy and affection of family members and others toward its possessor.
4. Life is conceived as sacred in terms of its place in a categorical moral or religious order of rights and duties.
5. Life is valued both in terms of its relation to community welfare and in terms of life being a universal human right.
6. Belief in the sacredness of human life as representing a universal human value of respect for the individual.

I have called this scheme a typology. This is because about 50 per cent of most people's thinking will be at a single stage, regardless of the moral dilemma involved. We call our types *stages* because they seem to represent an *invariant developmental sequence*. "True" stages come one at a time and always in the same order.

All movement is forward in sequence, and does not skip steps. Children may move through these stages at varying speeds, of course, and may be found half in and half out of a particular stage. An individual may stop at any given stage and at any age, but if he continues to move, he must move in accord with these steps. Moral reasoning of the conventional or Stage 3-4 kind never occurs before the preconventional Stage-1 and Stage-2 thought has taken place. No adult in Stage 4 has gone through Stage 6, but all Stage-6 adults have gone at least through 4.

While the evidence is not complete, my study strongly suggests that moral change fits the stage pattern just described. (The major uncertainty is whether all Stage 6s go through Stage 5 or whether these are two alternate mature orientations.)

How Values Change

As a single example of our findings of stage-sequence, take the progress of two boys on the aspect "The Value of Human Life." The first boy, Tommy, is asked "Is it better to save the life of one important person or a lot of unimportant people?" At age 10, he answers "all the people that aren't important because one man just has one house, maybe a lot of furniture, but a whole bunch of people have an awful lot of furniture and some of these poor people might have a lot of money and it doesn't look it."

Clearly Tommy is Stage 1: he confuses the value of a human being with the value of the property he possesses. Three years later (age 13) Tommy's conceptions of life's value are most clearly elicited by the question, "Should the doctor 'mercy kill' a fatally ill woman requesting death because of her pain?" He answers, "Maybe it would be good to put her out of her pain, she'd be better off that way. But the husband wouldn't want it, it's not like an animal. If a pet dies you can get along without it—it isn't something you really need. Well, you can get a new wife, but it's not really the same."

Here his answer is Stage 2: the value of the woman's life is partly contingent on its hedonistic value to the wife herself but even more contingent on its instrumental value to her husband, who can't replace her as easily as he can a pet.

Three years later still (age 16) Tommy's conception of life's value is elicited by the same question, to which he replies: "It might be best for her, but her husband—it's a human life—not like an animal; it just doesn't have the same relationship that a human being does to a family. You can become attached to a dog, but nothing like a human you know."

Now Tommy has moved from a Stage 2 instrumental view of the woman's value to a Stage-3 view based on the husband's distinctively human empathy and love for someone in his family. Equally clearly, it lacks any basis for a universal human value of the woman's life, which would hold if she had no husband or if her husband didn't love her. Tommy, then, has moved step by step through three stages during the age 10-16. Tommy, though bright (I.Q. 120), is a slow developer in moral judgment. Let us take another boy, Richard, to show us sequential movement through the remaining three steps.

At age 13, Richard said about the mercy-killing, "If she requests it, it's really up to her. She is in such terrible pain, just the same as people are always putting animals out of their pain," and in general showed a mixture of Stage-2 and Stage-3 responses concerning the value of life. At 16, he said, "I don't know. In one way, it's murder, it's not a right or privilege of man to decide who shall live and who should die. God put life into everybody on earth and you're taking away something from that person that came directly from God, and you're destroying something that is very sacred, it's in a way part of God and it's almost destroying a part of God when you kill a person. There's something of God in everyone."

Here Richard clearly displays a Stage-4 concept of life as sacred in terms of its place in a categorical moral or religious order. The value of human life is universal, it is true for all humans. It is still, however, dependent on something else, upon respect for God and God's authority; it is not an autonomous human value. Presumably if God told Richard to murder, as God commanded Abraham to murder Isaac, he would do so.

At age 20, Richard said to the same question: "There are more and more people in the medical profession who think it is a hardship on everyone, the person, the family, when you know they are going to die. When a person is kept alive by an artificial lung or kidney it's more like being a vegetable than being a human. If it's her own choice, I think there are certain rights and privileges that go along with being a human being. I am a human being and have certain desires for life and I think everybody else does too. You have a world of which you are the center, and everybody else does too and in that sense we're all equal."

Richard's response is clearly Stage 5, in that the value of life is defined in terms of equal and universal human rights in a context of relativity ("You have a world of which you are the center and in that sense we're all equal"), and of concern for utility or welfare consequences.

The Final Step

At 24, Richard says: "A human life takes precedence over any other moral or legal value, whoever it is. A human life has inherent value whether or not it is valued by a particular individual. The worth of the individual human being is central where the principles of justice and love are normative for all human relationships."

This young man is at Stage 6 in seeing the value of human life as absolute in representing a universal and equal respect for the human as an individual. He has moved step by step through a sequence culminating in a definition of human life as centrally valuable rather than derived from or dependent on social or divine authority.

In a genuine and culturally universal sense, these steps lead toward an increased *morality* of value judgment, where morality is considered as a form of judging, as it has been in a philosophic tradition running from the analyses of Kant to those of the modern analytic or "ordinary language" philosophers. The person at Stage 6 has disentangled his judgments of—or language about—human life from status and property values (Stage 1), from its uses to others (Stage 2), from interpersonal affection (Stage 3), and so on; he has a means of moral judgment that is universal and impersonal. The Stage-6 person's answers use moral words like "duty" or "morally right," and he uses them in a way implying universality, ideals, impersonality: He thinks and speaks in phrases like "regardless of who it was," or ". . . I would do it in spite of punishment."

Across Cultures

When I first decided to explore moral development in other cultures, I was told by anthropologist friends that I would have to throw away my culture-bound moral concepts and stories and start from scratch learning a whole new set of values for each new culture. My first try consisted of a brace of villages, one Atayal (Malaysian aboriginal) and the other Taiwanese.

My guide was a young Chinese ethnographer who had written an account of the moral and religious patterns of the Atayal and Taiwanese villages. Taiwanese boys in the 10-13 age group were asked about a story involving theft of food. A man's wife is starving to death but the store owner won't give the man any food unless he can pay, which he can't. Should he break in and steal some food? Why? Many of the boys said, "He should steal the food for his wife because if she dies he'll have to pay for her funeral and that costs a lot."

My guide was amused by these responses, but I was relieved: they were of course "classic" Stage-2 responses. In the Atayal village, funerals weren't such a big thing, so the Stage-2 boys would say, "He should steal the food because he needs his wife to cook for him."

This means that we need to consult our anthropologists to know what content a Stage-2 child will include in his instrumental exchange calculations, or what a Stage-4 adult will identify as the proper social order. But one certainly doesn't have to start from scratch. What made my guide laugh was the difference in form between the children's Stage-2 thought and his own, a difference definable independently of particular cultures.

Illustrations number 1 and number 2 indicate the cultural universality of the sequence of stages which we have found. Illustration number 1 presents the age trends for middle-class urban boys in the U.S., Taiwan and Mexico. At age 10 in each country, the order of use of each stage is the same as the order of its difficulty or maturity.

In the United States, by age 16 the order is the reverse, from the highest to the lowest, except that Stage 6 is still little-used. At age 13, the good-boy, middle stage (Stage 3), is [most] used.

The results in Mexico and Taiwan are the same, except that development is a little slower. The most conspicuous feature is that at the age of 16, Stage-5 thinking is much more salient in the United States than in Mexico or Taiwan. Nevertheless, it *is* present in the other countries, so we know that this is not purely an American democratic construct.

Illustration 2 shows strikingly similar results from two isolated villages, one in Yucatan, one in Turkey. While conventional moral thought increases steadily from ages 10 to 16 it still has not achieved a clear ascendency over pre-conventional thought.

Trends for lower-class urban groups are intermediate in the rate of development between those for the middle-class and for the village boys. In the three divergent cultures that I studied, middle-class children were found to be more advanced in moral judgment than matched lower-class children. This was not due to the fact that the middle-class children heavily favored some one type of thought which could be seen as corresponding to the prevailing middle-class pattern. Instead, middle-class and working-class children move through the same sequences, but the middle-class children move faster and farther.

This sequence is not dependent upon a particular religion, or any religion at all in the usual sense. I found no important differences in the

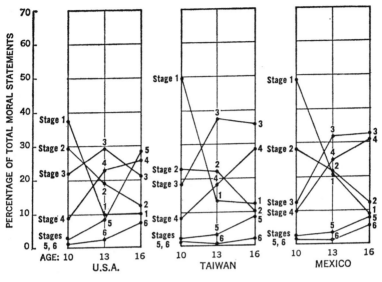

1. *Middle-class urban boys in the U.S., Taiwan and Mexico (above). At age 10 the stages are used according to difficulty. At age 13, Stage 3 is most used by all three groups. At age 16 U.S. boys have reversed the order of age 10 stages (with the exception of 6). In Taiwan and Mexico, conventional (3-4) stages prevail at age 16, with Stage 5 also little used.*

2. *Two isolated villages, one in Turkey, the other in Yucatan, show similar patterns in moral thinking. There is no reversal of order, and preconventional (1-2) thought does not gain a clear ascendancy over conventional stages at age 16.*

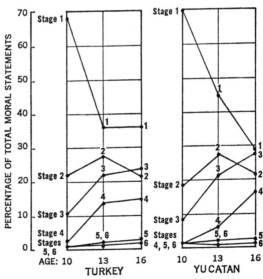

development of moral thinking among Catholics, Protestants, Jews, Buddhists, Moslems and atheists. Religious values seem to go through the same stages as all other values.

Trading Up

In summary, the nature of our sequence is not significantly affected by widely varying social, cultural or religious conditions. The only thing that is affected is the *rate* at which individuals progress through this sequence.

Why should there be such a universal invariant sequence of development? In answering this question, we need first to analyze these developing social concepts in terms of their internal logical structure. At each stage, the same basic moral concept or aspect is defined, but at each higher stage this definition is more differentiated, more integrated and more general or universal. When one's concept of human life moves from Stage 1 to Stage 2 the value of life becomes more differentiated from the value of property, more integrated (the value of life enters an organizational hierarchy where it is "higher" than property so that one steals property in order to save life) and more universalized (the life of any sentient being is valuable regardless of status or property). The same advance is true at each stage in the hierarchy. Each step of development then is a better cognitive organization than the one before it, one which takes account of everything present in the previous stage, but making new distinctions and organizing them into a more comprehensive or more equilibrated structure. The fact that this is the case has been demonstrated by a series of studies indicating that children and adolescents comprehend all stages up to their own, but not more than one stage beyond their own. And importantly, *they prefer this next stage.*

We have conducted experimental moral discussion classes which show that the child at an earlier stage of development tends to move forward when confronted by the views of a child one stage further along. In an argument between a Stage-3 and Stage-4 child, the child in the third stage tends to move toward or into Stage 4, while the Stage-4 child understands but does not accept the arguments of the Stage-3 child.

Moral thought, then, seems to behave like all other kinds of thought. Progress through the moral levels and stages is characterized by increasing differentiation and increasing integration, and hence is the same kind of progress that scientific theory represents. Like acceptable scientific theory—or like *any* theory or structure of knowledge—moral thought may be considered partially to generate its own data as it goes along, or at least to expand so as to contain in a balanced, self-consistent way a wider and wider experimental field. The raw data in the case of our ethical philosophies may be considered as conflicts between roles, or values, or as the social order in which men live.

The Role of Society

The social worlds of all men seem to contain the same basic structures. All the societies we have studied have the same basic institutions —family, economy, law, government. In addition, however, all societies are alike because they *are* societies—systems of defined complementary roles. In order to *play* a social role in the family, school or society, the child must implicitly take the role of others toward himself and toward others in the group. These role-taking tendencies form the basis of all social institutions. They represent various patternings of shared or complementary expectations.

In the preconventional and conventional levels (Stages 1-4), moral content or value is largely accidental or culture-bound. Anything from "honesty" to "courage in battle" can be the central value. But in the higher postconventional levels, Socrates, Lincoln, Thoreau and Martin Luther King tend to speak without confusion of tongues, as it were. This is because the ideal principles of any social structure are basically alike, if only because there simply aren't that many principles which are articulate, comprehensive and integrated enough to be satisfying to the human intellect. And most of these principles have gone by the name of justice.

Behavioristic psychology and psychoanalysis have always upheld the Philistine view that fine moral words are one thing and moral deeds another. Morally mature reasoning is quite a different matter, and does not really depend on "fine words." The man who understands justice is more likely to practice it.

In our studies, we have found that youths who understand justice act more justly, and the man who understands justice helps create a moral climate which goes far beyond his immediate and personal acts. The universal society is the beneficiary.

PART FIVE

Teaching
and Morality

In Part Four we focused our attention on the centrality of moral thinking and autonomy for the notion of moral man and moral education. The thrust of the argument was that vis-à-vis morality a person's thinking, intentions, and choosing are as important as his behaviors. Such a position is corrective of overly behavior-centered notions of morality and moral education. Still it would be naive to regard thinking, intentions, and choosing as *the* criteria of morality. Ultimately, the moral sphere is a realm of actions and consequences of actions. While a society of thinking and choosing agents is an important ideal, there is also the possibility that such a society might be a terribly disorderly or even self-destructive phenomenon. For the uncomfortable fact is that while moral thinking is a key aspect of the *meaning* of the concept "morality," it does not always generate moral behaviors in the *reality* of human existence. In short, "autonomous" people may frequently choose immoral actions.

The potential gap between moral thinking and moral behaviors is one of the problematic issues in both moral life and moral education. On the one hand, the philosophers claim that moral life encompasses freely evaluated and chosen judgments; on the other hand, the realities of social life demand a certain level of acceptable moral behavior. In addition, there is no guarantee that the person who has been taught to think about and understand moral issues, and even to make moral decisions, *will* in practice think about and make moral decisions, let alone the correct moral decisions. There is even less a guarantee that he will always choose behaviors deemed desirable by society. The issue in question, then, is the gap between knowing what is right (moral knowledge) and doing it (moral action).

William Frankena attempts to solve this paradox by postulating two parallel functions of moral education: MEX, the handing on of a "knowledge of good and evil"; and MEY, the ensuring that our children's conduct will conform to this "knowledge." His argument is that these two activities are indispensable, correlated subcategories of the enterprise of "moral education" whereby society both educates intelligent moral agents and guarantees socially acceptable moral behavior. Frankena's claim is that these two processes are interrelated and may be implemented concurrently.

Archambault considers the complexity of the task for moral education, in terms of relating moral understanding to moral conduct, in the domain of schooling. His claim is that such a conception implies a broader and more comprehensive notion of the school as an institution responsible for both intellectual processes and moral conduct. That is, if the transition from moral knowledge to moral action is not automatic, then the school must be specifically concerned with both the intellectual and the behavioral aspects of moral life. Archambault's argument is not that moral education, especially in the sense of moral conduct, must become *the* focus of schooling. Rather, his contention is that schools should be sensitive to those "moral" intellectual and behavioral skills which can be developed within the existing framework of the school curriculum. The assertion here is that the school has certain clearly defined functions and contents, *some of which* are relevant and utilizable for the enterprise of moral education but only if they are recognized as such.

Our analysis of major themes of moral philosophy has led us to a much broader and also more cumbersome picture of moral education. At this point, the educator must resign himself to the conclusion that, for all their convenience, simplistic definitions of "moral education" are hazardous. We have seen that moral education cannot be simplistically categorized as either behavioral training, attitude development, or training in the moral thinking processes. Instead, moral education must be treated as a multifaceted activity encompassing several constituent educational objectives. The concern of moral education, then, is to deal with these respective educational objectives as well as to show the way in which all these elements unite to constitute the moral life. The final selection, by Raths, Harmin, and Simon, attempts such a practical synthesis.

XIII

*Toward a Philosophy of Moral Education**
WILLIAM K. FRANKENA

The topic of moral education has had a great deal of attention from educators during the last few decades, sometimes under the unlovely label of "character education" and sometimes under the confused and confusing caption of "moral and spiritual values." Yet, as some of these educators themselves insist, ". . . the present character education movement is uncertain as to theory, . . . not sure of its direction."[1] . . .

*   *   *

In what follows, therefore, I shall cover the ground usually traversed in studies of moral education, trying as a philosopher to clarify the tasks involved in teaching morality to our children, but without saying much about the methods by which they are to be accomplished. My point will be that moral education includes teaching, learning and espousing, not only a particular morality, but the very art or idea of morality itself.

I

Socrates and his contemporaries conceived of the problem of moral education as that of teaching "virtue," and Socrates at least was troubled

---

*Reprinted with permission of author and publisher from *Harvard Educational Review*, Vol. 28 (Fall 1958), pp. 300-313. Copyright © 1958 by President and Fellows of Harvard College.

[1]Betts, G. H. and G. E. Hill, as quoted by H. C. McKown, *Character Education* (New York: McGraw-Hill, 1935), p. 12.

148

about the method and even the possibility of teaching this, on the ground that the most virtuous parents so often have vicious sons (he did not seem to be worried about daughters). Preachers' sons are too often wicked, and psychologists' sons too often maladjusted. In short, parent-generations have not succeeded in ensuring the conformity to their standards of the conduct of their offspring. Suppose we similarly conceive the problem as that of producing in our children the kind of behavior that we call virtuous. Now Socrates, since he held that we always do what we think right, thought the problem was simply that of passing on a knowledge or true opinion about what is virtuous. If we can do this, he thought, we can secure the future. But most subsequent moral philosophy has doubted the "Socratic paradox" (although much recent educational philosophy does seem to imply a similar optimism about human nature). It has not been persuaded that knowledge is enough, even though it may not agree that love is enough either. We may perhaps take for granted, then, that the problem of producing virtue in the next generation is a twofold one: (1) that of handing on a "knowledge of good and evil" or "knowing how" to act, and (2) that of ensuring that our children's conduct will conform to this "knowledge." For convenience I shall call these two tasks respectively Moral Education X and Moral Education Y, referring to them familiarly as MEX and MEY.

*   *   *

II

MEX cannot consist of a long list of specific instructions to our children for all of the situations into which they may fall. It must consist, rather, in teaching them certain principles or ends by which they may guide their conduct in those situations. For teaching these rules or ends either the direct or the indirect methods may be used. That is, we may formulate the rules or ends quite explicitly and seek to inculcate them into our children. . . . Or we may tell our children or otherwise instruct them, perhaps by example, what to do in this particular case and in that particular case until they begin to discern the rule or the end involved for themselves. Either way, the point is to teach them ends or principles, "that they may do them in the land which I the Lord shall give them", for, like Moses, we shall not be there to lead them.

Yet the point of moral instruction *is* to put the child in the position of being able to decide what he should do in each situation he may come up against; and, for this, it is necessary but not sufficient to teach him the ends or principles involved. We must also supply him with the knowledge required to apply the principle or to realize the end in question, or with the ability to acquire this knowledge for himself. Roughly speaking, as Aristotle and many others have pointed out, the process of determining what one should do takes the form of a "practical syllogism". There is (a) the rule or end, for example, that of keeping one's promises or of not harming anyone. There is (b) the factual knowledge that one has tacitly or openly made a certain promise, or that certain actions will cause harm to certain people. And there is (c) the conclusion that one should or should not do a certain deed. Thus, if our children are to be able to come to right conclusions about what to do, they must have or be able to get the kind of factual knowledge involved in (b). This means that their moral education must include a training in history and science; we must teach them whatever we know that may be relevant to the solution of their moral problems, and train them to go on to find out whatever more they need to know....

*   *   *

So far, however, we have been supposing that the problem in MEX is simply to pass on a set of moral principles which is adequate for all occasions, provided only that we also pass on the knowledge and the intelligence needed to apply them. Actually the problem is much more complex than this.

(1) Whether we use the direct or the indirect method of moral instruction, we can do so in either of two ways. We can simply "internalize" in our children certain beliefs about how to act, without any indication of any reasons which may lie behind them. That is, we might conceive of moral education in a "Theirs not to reason why" spirit and we might even use such techniques as drill, propaganda, and hidden persuasion. On the other hand, we might take the position that we must teach the reasons as well as the conclusions. Now, there is, no doubt, a period in the life of a child when such appeals to reason are pointless. Says Felix Adler, "The right to reason about these matters cannot be conceded until after the mind has attained a certain maturity. . . . The moral teacher . . . is not to explain [to the child] why we should do the

right. . . ."[2] Plato agreed, and thought it the function of a proper education in poetry and music to use this period in schooling the youth to approve what is to be approved and condemn what is to be condemned, "while he is still too young to understand the reason," that "when reason comes, he will greet her as a friend with whom his education has made him long familiar."[3] The question is not whether the introduction of reasons is to begin at birth, but whether it is to begin as soon as it is feasible or is to be put off as long as it can be, perhaps forever.

*   *   *

Now, most recent educational philosophy has insisted on the importance in moral as well as in other education of developing and appealing to the child's reason whenever possible. With this I agree, at least to the extent of believing that a reference to reasons in morality must be made in the schools, even if criticism and moral philosophy are to be put off until college, as Aristotle thought. For, as recent ethical writers have been pointing out, it is the very genius of morality to appeal to reason. To make a moral judgment is to claim that it is justified, that a case can be made for it. . . . Thus, if the parent, speaking as a moral being, says, "You ought to do so and so," it is appropriate for the child to ask, "Why?", and the parent must be prepared, as soon as the child can understand, with some kind of answer, and not just with any kind of answer but with one which will indicate to him what reasons are supposed to count in morality. R. S. Peters even goes so far as to say, in criticizing Freud, "But customary and obsessive behavior is not morality, for by 'morality' we mean *at least* the intelligent following of rules the point of which is understood."[4]

This point may be pushed a bit farther. It is characteristic of a moral judgment, not only to imply reasons, but to claim a basis in considerations of fact which are objectively valid.[5] Hence the reasons adduced by a teacher must not be recognizable to the pupil as mere propaganda calculated to win his assent; they must be such as will bear

[2]Adler, F., *The Moral Instruction of Children* (New York: D. Appleton, 1901), pp. 13-15.
[3]*Republic,* 402a.
[4]Peters, R. S., *The Concept of Motivation* (London: Routledge, 1958), p. 87.
[5]See M. Mandelbaum, *The Phenomenology of Moral Experience* (Glencoe: Free Press, 1955), pp. 243-57.

whatever investigation the pupil may make, else his adherence to the moral enterprise and his virtue will alike be jeopardized.

*   *   *

This means that we parent-teachers must ourselves have some sense of the rationale of moral commands, and for this we may well go to the moral philosophers, even if our children are to be held back from doing so. We must be prepared, however, to find that they disagree profoundly among themselves about what this rationale is, and, while we can learn much from them, we shall have to a considerable extent to rely on what Rice calls our own "global sense of directedness" which was made a part of our "second nature" by our own teachers and "by long buffeting from the world," [6] and without which we shall not be able to benefit from the study of moral philosophy anyway.

(2) The need of building this global sense of moral direction into the second nature of the next generation is reinforced by another consideration, namely, the occurrence of conflicts of duties. Unless the morality which we propose to teach our children is unusually circumspect, it will contain principles which may come into conflict in their experience. In fact, most practical moral problems consist, not simply in applying a given principle, but in resolving conflicts between principles, as in the tragic case of Antigone or in Sartre's example of the young man who "was faced with the choice of leaving for England and joining the Free French Forces . . . or remaining with his mother and helping her to carry on." [7] In such situations, one has one's learned stock of principles. One has also, let us suppose, a well-trained intellect and an excellent supply of relevant information. But, using this information and this intelligence, one still finds a conflict between principles P and Q. If one has also been taught another principle, R, which gives P precedence over Q, all is well, but this is not always the case. Then one must make what Hare calls a "decision of principle"—one must somehow formulate a rule for dealing with the situation in question. This means that we must not only teach our principles and the knowledge required to apply them, but must also prepare the younger generation for a certain creativeness or originality in soving moral problems. We

[6] Cf. Rice, P. B., *On the Knowledge of Good and Evil* (New York: Random House, 1955), pp. 186, 190f., 194f.
[7] Sartre, J-P., *Existentialism* (New York: Philosophical Library, 1947), p. 29.

must somehow give them the ability to decide what to do when the answer does not follow from principles learned together with relevant factual information.

(3) This same ability is called for in dealing with another exigency with which new generations are often faced—that of revising or abandoning learned principles in the light of new situations and new knowledge or insight. Perhaps the Socratic-Christian doctrine that it is never right to harm even one's enemies can be regarded as such a revision of a previous rule, or the more recent view that punishment is not retributive but prospective or therapeutic in function. Other reformulations of long-accepted principles may be forced on us by recent work in depth or in social psychology, or even by developments in biophysics. And, unless we mean to leave this sort of moral reform entirely to fortune and sporadic genius, we must try to prepare our successors to sense when such a revision of principle is called for and along what lines.

From these considerations it follows that with all our giving of principles we must give understanding and initiative. We must, in teaching principles, try to communicate a sense of their rationale, and along with this a sense of the direction in which to look in cases of conflict or in the event of radically new knowledge or situation; and, at the same time, as Hare emphasizes, we must provide "ample opportunity of making the decisions—by which [principles] are modified, improved, adapted to changed circumstances, or even abandoned if they become entirely unsuited to a new environment."[8] To do this will not be easy for us, for our own generation seems not to have been adequately prepared by its parent-teachers for coping with the changes which have occurred and are occurring. Our own moral education has been wanting either on the side of moral direction or on the side of opportunity for moral decision or both—as well as in the matter of relevant intellectual discipline and factual knowledge. Else neither the existentialism nor the medievalism which we have with us could have arisen.

(4) There is a fourth complication in the program I am calling MEX, one which is implicit in the three just discussed, namely, that of rearing autonomous moral agents. This notion of autonomy is a difficult one. It seems clear that morality is a guide to life of a peculiar sort in that it allows the individual to be, indeed insists on his being, self-

[8]Hare, R. M., *The Language of Morals* (Oxford: Clarendon, 1952), p. 76.

governed in the sense, not only of determining what he is going to do, but of determining what it is that he should do. This feature of morality has been stressed by Kant, Durkheim, and many recent writers. In some of the recent writers, however, this autonomy of the individual is misconstrued; it is taken to mean that the individual can create his own standards, and that there is no sort of authority which he must respect. This is the well-known view of Sartre, but something like it seems to be implied by Nowell-Smith when he concludes his book by saying,

> The most a moral philosopher can do is to paint a picture of various types of life . . . and ask which type of life you really want to lead. . . . The questions 'what shall I do?' and 'what moral principles should I adopt?' must be answered by each man for himself; that at least is part of the connotation of the word 'moral.' [9]

But to say that a developed moral agent must make up his own mind what is right, and not simply accept the dictates of an external authority, is not to say that he can make a course of action right by deciding on it, or that whatever life he chooses or prefers to live can be claimed by him to be *ipso facto* morally right or good; any more than to say that a developed rational man must make up his own mind what is true, and not merely accept the declarations of another, is to say that he can make a statement true by believing it, or that whatever system he chooses or prefers to believe can be claimed by him to be *ipso facto* intellectually justified. Being autonomous does not mean being responsible to no transpersonal standard in morality any more than in science. In both cases one is involved in an interpersonal enterprise of human guidance (in morality of action, in science of belief) in which one is self-governing but in which one makes judgments ("This is right", "That is true") which one is claiming to be warranted by a review of the facts from the impersonal standpoint represented by that enterprise and shared by all who take part in it—a claim which is not merely an assertion of what one chooses or prefers, and may turn out to be mistaken.

In morality, then, as in science, we must impart to those who come after us a certain difficult but qualified independence or self-reliance of judgment. This and the other three complications in the

[9]Nowell-Smith, P. H., *Ethics* (Melbourne: Penguin, 1954), p. 319f; cf. Hare, *op. cit.,* p. 77f.

problem of MEX, however, add up to much the same thing—that there
is a Moral Direction or Way which transcends the individual, and
within which he stands or claims to stand on his own feet when he
makes moral judgments which are not second-hand. . . . This Way is for
each generation more or less embodied in a set of rules, principles,
ideals, or virtues, and this set is what it must proceed to teach to the
next generation; but moral education does not consist simply in passing
it on intact. Its important task is, rather, in and through the teaching
of these ideals or rules, to instill a sense of the Way or Point of View
which is involved in morality, and to prepare its pupils to stay self-
reliantly within this Way even when the map we have been using turns
out to be unclear or inaccurate.

III

*   *   *

. . . With this, our discussion of MEX has completed its course,
and we may take a look at MEY. We must be relatively brief about
this, and that is regrettable, for MEY, like the month when this was
written or any beautiful woman of the same name, is always an interesting subject.

The object of this part of moral education is to keep the youth
from replying, "I can but I won't", when Duty whispers low, "Thou
must." In W. T. Harris' words, where the job of MEX is "the formation of right ideas," that of MEY is "the formation of right habits,"[10]
that is, the developing of dispositions which will lead one both to ask
what the right is and to act accordingly. First among such dispositions
are the moral virtues. These, as Aristotle held, are habits of using the
"intellectual virtue" or ability developed in MEX to determine what
is right, and of choosing it deliberately because it is right. They are of
two kinds. There are somewhat restricted first-order ones such as honesty and veracity; and there are more general second-order ones such
as conscientiousness, integrity, and moral alertness. Both kinds are
acquired by practice; as Aristotle said, "we become just by doing just acts,
temperate by doing temperate acts, brave by doing brave acts."[11] Character education, properly so-called, which must be part of what Professor

[10]Editor's Preface to Adler, *op. cit.*, p. v.
[11]*Nicomachean Ethics*, II, i, 4.

Ducasse calls education of the will, consists of thus building into the young such dispositions as these.

*   *   *

In addition to cultivating these "internal sanctions" of morality, as Mill called them, MEY can also make use of such "external sanctions" as punishment or reward (legal, parental, or scholastic) and praise or blame. These are all means of keeping young people on the straight and narrow path, not by changing their motivations, but by using those they already have....

*   *   *

I shall, however, stick to general theory and not try to evaluate the use of specific kinds of external sanctions. They are all ways of *making* it to an individual's interest to do what is or is regarded as right by some sort of *ad hoc* action, and, while it is clear that morality would like to make its way without them, it is not easy to see how moral education and guidance can get on without anything of the sort. How else, for instance, can it secure the kind of practice which Aristotle says is necessary to produce the habits of justice and temperance, especially when reason cannot yet be used and emulation and generosity do not suffice? We may give up punishment and reward, and limit ourselves to the use of such expressions as "You did right," "But that would be wrong," or "Good boys don't do things like that," but even then we are not simply instructing, we are also appealing to the relishes of esteem and disgrace. This is a sanction which seems almost to be inherent in the use of moral language, and, indeed, Bentham calls it "the moral sanction." That is part of the reason why some contemporary philosophers have been able to make so much of the "emotive meaning" of ethical terms.[12]

Another technique which moralists have often used is not to *make* virtue profitable in this way but rather to *show* that it is profitable or make people *believe* that it is—to prove to the individual or otherwise lead him to believe, that the world is so constituted as to visit his iniquity, not only on his children and his children's children unto the fourth generation of them that hate morality, but on him. Here enter many gambits which I cannot recite but which are familiar to readers

[12]E. g. C. L. Stevenson, *Ethics and Language* (New Haven: Yale University Press, 1944).

of Plato, Butler, and Hume, as well as of more ordinary moral literature, among them the religious appeal to punishments and rewards in a hereafter. Which of these are sound arguments and which involve what Bergson called myth-making I shall not try to determine. Like Professor Ducasse, I am not convinced that a religious sanction in the form indicated is necessary to morality, and in any case it cannot be appealed to in our public schools. Moreover, I believe that any attempt to prove that being virtuous is always profitable to every individual is and must remain inconclusive, thought it may go a long way. But, for so far as it goes, I see no reason why such an attempt should not be included as a part of MEY, at least when it relies on honest argument and not on propaganda—provided that it is not construed as an attempt to give a justification for what is claimed to be right but only as a way of securing the motivation for doing it. Even then, however, it must be made carefully, for the cause of morality will be endangered if the individual is led to think that virtue's promise of profit is its only inducement. That virtue is its own reward is a hoary adage, but it has a present meaning.

Whatever the methods used in MEY, its main concern must not be merely that the individual shall be disposed to act in accordance with certain principles or ideals of right and wrong which have been taught to him in MEX. As the final goal in MEX must be to get across an understanding of the Moral Way and its direction, so the final goal in MEY must be to dispose the individual to follow this Way in spite of contrary temptations, conflicts of duty, or novel situations. Plato thought that we invariably pursue the Idea of the Good, and that our only problem (and hope) in moral education is to understand this Idea or gain true opinion from someone who does. But perhaps there is no such Idea of the *Good* which we can come out of the Cave one day to know in all its glory, and perhaps our problem is rather to understand the Idea of *Morality* as a kind human guidance and to bring about a devotion to it (for such understanding and devotion hardly seem to be natural). It is here that MEX and MEY meet and marry, for of course they are of opposite sexes and bound to fall in love at first sight.

This means that, as MEX must not be occupied simply with teaching a specific set of principles like truth-telling and promise-keeping, but especially with developing a "global sense of moral directedness," and an *ability* to think objectively and impartially, so MEY must not be wholly concerned with developing first-order dispositions like hon-

esty, but more generally with cultivating such second order dispositions as integrity, self-control, and a *readiness* to be governed by impartial and objective thinking and fact-finding.

In saying all this I have been talking as if MEX and MEY are two
independent programs of education which meet only at the end. And,
indeed, they are distinct and must not be confused. But, of course, they
are just two aspects or parts of a single process of moral education,
which is going on all the time (just as moral education as a whole is
an aspect or part of a yet larger single process of total education), and
which has a single ideal of which theirs are components. Really MEX
and MEY do not get together only at the end; they are in love and married all the time. Any actual program of moral education must con-
secrate this marriage at every step, though it must also remember which
is husband and which wife.

                          *   *   *

So much for the goals or tasks of moral education as a philosopher
sees them. I have not said much about methods. This is mainly a matter
for psychologists and educational scientists, though I may add that such
philosophers as Russell have much to say here that is helpful. One
general remark I must make, namely, that the methods of moral education must be moral. That is, the actions of parents and teachers in
dealing with children and pupils must themselves be right by moral
standards. Because the end is virtue it does not follow that every means
is justified. In fact, the use of immoral means is certain to preclude the
realization of the end when the end is morality.

Little also has been said to help solve in any specific way the problem of "the early corruption of youth," as Locke called it, which has been
the burden of complaint of every parent-generation since Adam or at
least since Hesiod. Indeed, I doubt that this is a matter in which
philosophers have any special competence; even moral philosophers must
leave it largely to parents, churches, schools, and psychologists. Even
with all these doing their best within the framework of what has been
said here, the motto of moral education must always be that of the
Michigan football teams of yesteryear—"Punt, pass, and pray." It is
part of the essence of morality, as of democracy and the American system of education, to run the risk of failure. . . .

XIV

Criteria for Success in Moral Instruction*
REGINALD D. ARCHAMBAULT

This paper is prompted by Israel Scheffler's treatment of "teaching and telling" in his recent book *The Language of Education*.[1] In that analysis he draws distinctions that are crucial to an adequate discussion of what is involved in moral instruction, distinctions which prompt further inquiry and raise many important questions. Professor Scheffler ends his book with the suggestion that some problems that he discusses need further exploration. This paper is an attempt to explore one of them. One major issue that arises from his analysis is the delineation of the school's role and responsibility with regard to moral instruction, and, more basically, an adequate definition of "moral instruction" and a description of what this involves.

Scheffler demonstrates that there are many ambiguities in the concept of moral education, some of which are the result of a peculiar linguistic ambiguity involved in norm-stating sentences. The ambiguity results from the fact that there are two possible interpretations of "teaching that" statements. The example used is: "X taught Y that honesty is the best policy."[2] This sentence can be given an active or a

*Reprinted with permission of author and publisher from *Harvard Educational Review*, Vol. 33 (Fall 1963), pp. 472-483. Copyright © 1963 by President and Fellows of Harvard College.
[1] *The Language of Education*, Springfield, Ill., Charles C Thomas, 1960, pp. 77-101.
[2] *Ibid.*, pp. 78ff.

non-active interpretation. In a *non-active* interpretation, for X to be successful in teaching Y that honesty is the best policy, Y should need to demonstrate that he had learned the statement and that he believed it, but *acting* honestly would not be an index of success. Thus the test given to determine success in teaching that honesty is the best policy, in its non-active interpretation, would be similar to the test given to determine whether or not X was successful in teaching Y that Columbus discovered America. On the other hand, it is possible to give an *active* interpretation of norm-stating sentences so that success in teaching that honesty is the best policy would be determined by examining Y's conduct in certain situations where the norm of honesty could be invoked and acted upon. Scheffler's major point is that since this basic ambiguity exists, it is possible to shift between the two interpretations with the most undesirable practical results. We may begin with an active interpretation of such norm-stating sentences, shift in the process of instruction and test to a non-active interpretation, and finally presume that we have been successful in moral instruction in the *active* sense, whereas we have actually taught and tested for knowledge as interpreted in a non-active sense.

Scheffler's analysis is most helpful in clarifying a basic ambiguity that bears directly on problems of moral education. When it is taken together with other subtle distinctions that he makes between types of knowing and teaching, it gives us a series of important insights as well as a method for treating certain crucial issues involved in moral education. It does not give us an indication or suggestion as to a desirable and reasonable interpretation of the role of the teacher in moral instruction, and of the criteria for his success in such instruction, although there seem to be indications of Scheffler's views on these matters. These issues will now concern us here.

The "aims" of instruction are usually stated vaguely. They often exist as a facade behind which the actual process of instruction can go on undisturbed. If we want a true indication of what the aims of instruction are in any given course, we must look to the examinations that are given to the students, and to the criteria used by teachers for measuring success on the examinations. If we are engaged in teaching "critical thinking," "art appreciation," or "moral conduct" we can get a clue as to the actual working definition of these terms as well as the actual aims of instruction by looking at the knowledge or behavior that students are expected to exhibit on the successful completion of such a course. In this way we can determine the actual aims or content of instruction. It is for this reason that the postulation of criteria for success is a crucial consideration in all teaching, but particularly in the ambiguous area of moral instruction. ...

* * *

What, then, should our aims be when we are engaged in moral instruction? The answer to this question would help us to delineate the responsibility of the school in this regard. Scheffler points out that it is a vague question because of the ambiguity of the term "moral instruction" and he helps to point out the sources of ambiguity, but he stops short of recommending a proper or reasonable answer.

The problem is complicated by the fact that we quite properly mean different things by "moral instruction" at different stages of the child's development. For example, if we are engaged in teaching a norm of honesty, we might construe it in these different ways,[3] depending on the maturity of the pupil:

(1) To teach Y to be honest through habit, using certain sanctions to insure honest behavior. (Training.)

(2) To teach Y that honesty is more desirable than dishonesty. (Teaching the rule and reasons for it.)

(3) To teach Y to believe in the rule that honesty is more desirable than dishonesty. (Teaching the student to reflect on the rule and to provide his own reasons for accepting it.)

(4) To teach Y to be honest out of conviction, and to ask him to offer objective and impartial reasons for this conviction. (Teaching the student to be committed to certain rules and to act in accordance with his convictions.)

The tests for success in each of these instances would be different. In (1) success would consist of Y's simply exhibiting a pattern of honest behavior; in (2) the test would determine whether Y could reproduce appropriate statements relative to the belief that honesty is a desirable norm; in (3) the acquisition of the belief itself would be tested by asking Y to give adequate reasons to support the belief; in (4) Y would be expected not only to give reasons for commitment to the belief, but evidence that he acts in accordance with the belief.

Each of these interpretations probably has a valid place in any program of moral instruction, for some might be considered prerequi-

[3]This schema is prompted by the Scheffler analysis, *ibid.*, pp. 94-95.

site to the later acquisition of knowledge or behavior deemed desirable and sufficient for success in moral instruction. The crucial question to be raised is: What are the minimal conditions sufficient to indicate success in moral instruction at the *end* of the teaching interval?

After reading the Scheffler analysis one might be tempted to construe this question in terms of deciding on an active *or* non-active interpretation of norm-stating sentences as a major clue to the definition of success. And at first blush, the answer would seem to be an easy one. To teach someone *about* honesty, or even to expect him to give reasons for holding that honesty is the best policy, would, after all, seem quite vacuous, since we have not taught and tested for moral conduct. Similarly, if we are successful in merely inculcating moral habits, there is no indication that this was done by having our students act out of conviction. We are tempted to conclude that moral instruction consists in the attempt to get students to acquire a norm or pattern of action, and to reflectively support these norms in an "objective" or "impartial" manner.[4] A necessary condition for success would then be the demonstration by the student of the appropriate moral behavior (acting honestly, paying one's debts, etc.). But this suggests a much more extensive responsibility for the school in insuring moral conduct. It suggests a much more "practical" environment where teaching and test were not "merely intellectual" and where students could demonstrate "actively" the successful acquisition of norms of conduct. The alternative would be to encourage mere verbalism, by turning out students whose beliefs are merely intellectual and unrelated to a pattern of action.

The dilemma is more apparent than real. As Scheffler suggests at one point in his analysis, the ambiguity involved in this discussion can be related to the classic problem of whether virtue can be taught. The crucial case is the one in which the student who demonstrates that he has been taught, in the non-active sense, that honesty is the best policy proceeds to act in ways incompatible with an adoption of the norm of honesty. Scheffler maintains that two interpretations of this case are possible, depending on one's position regarding the relation between knowledge and virtue. One would maintain that X had successfully taught Y, but that Y's failure to act on this knowledge can be attributed to a failure of the will. The other view would hold that the teaching

---

[4] See Scheffler, *ibid.,* p. 95.

has not been successful, since the appropriate moral conduct did not result.[5]

This points up the complexity of problems involved in deciding on the ends and means of moral instruction. Although Scheffler maintains that the problem of the relation between knowledge and virtue is "not as fundamental as it first appears" we soon see that it is the most basic issue to be dealt with in defining the aims of moral instruction, for the basic question here is the criterion for ascertaining success or failure in teaching. The choice is not arbitrary. We certainly have ample evidence to suggest that intellectual apprehension, understanding and avowal of norms do not guarantee an acquisition in conduct of the pattern of action prescribed by the norm. Since the transfer between belief and action is not automatic, the attainment of the aim of moral conduct must, then, involve not only intellectual apprehension and support of norms, but also a training of the will so that the student can bridge the gap between belief and action. This would make the task of moral intstruction much more complex.

It is thus that we arrive at the crucial question as to whether the responsibility of the school is to strive for success in the attainment of moral conduct on the part of its students. The answer to this, is I believe, a qualified "yes". As Scheffler points out, "the inculcation of habits, norms and propensities pervades all known educational practice,"[6] and teachers' responsibility for this cannot be evaded. It would seem to be true, then, that the school must assume some responsibility for promoting moral conduct. The more interesting question is the extent of this responsibility and precisely how this responsibility is to be fulfilled. Is it necessary to convert the school into a microcosm of society as the progressives would suggest, so that moral conduct in the school

[5]*Ibid.*, pp. 83-84. Traditionally, moral philosophers have held that moral training consists not only in leading the student to an intellectual apprehension of norms, but also in a training of the will. Aristotle, for example, emphasized the importance of habituation or practicing right acts, so that the student's will would be trained to do what his mind told him was right. William Frankena puts it this way: "We may perhaps take for granted, then, that the problem of producing virtue in the next generation is a twofold one: (1) that of handing on a 'knowledge of good and evil' or 'knowing how' to act, and (2) that of insuring that our children's conduct will conform to this 'knowledge'." "Toward a Philosophy of Moral Education," *Harvard Educational Review*, Fall, 1958, p. 302.

[6]Scheffler, *op. cit.*, p. 99.

mirrors that in the "world outside"? Must we have direct moral training such as we find in religious schools?

In order to answer these questions we must be clear as to what we mean by "moral conduct," so that we can see what would be involved in achieving it. Again we find Scheffler's analysis most helpful, for he points out that moral conduct does not consist merely in acting in accordance with a norm. Such behavior may come about through compulsion or force, or may be performed automatically. To be properly considered moral, conduct must entail a "reflective and impartial support of norms."[7] This involves, then, four factors, jointly sufficient to entail moral conduct: (a) belief in a norm; (b) a tendency and capacity to offer a rationale supporting the norm; (c) a disinterested or impartial application of judgment concerning the norm; and (d) a tendency and capacity to act in accordance with the norm. As teachers engaged in moral instruction we may strive to achieve any of these objectives. The manner in which we attempted to achieve them would probably differ in each case because of what is entailed by the objective itself. Nevertheless, as I have already suggested, we would be properly considered to be engaged in moral instruction at any of the levels listed. The crucial point is that if we aim to achieve moral conduct (d) as a result of our instruction, *all* of the above objectives must be met. Can this be accomplished within the framework of the school? Should it be?

I have suggested that striving for moral conduct is a qualified aim of the school. The school's responsibility is not to insure moral conduct, for such insurance is impossible. The school hopes that the student will achieve various kinds and degrees of understanding but it does not insure understanding. Rather, it makes available the means by which understanding can be acquired by presenting data, principles, and techniques to students, and testing for their success in learning these. It teaches for knowledge that promotes understanding. One of the conditions necessary for success in understanding rests with the pupil. We do not speak of failure in getting students to understand as a failure in teaching, unless our lesson has for some reason been incomplete. When we have offered a reasonable opportunity to the student to achieve understanding and he fails to do so, we attribute the failure to the pupil rather than to the instructors. Hence we say that we *promote* understanding rather than *teach* understanding. In this case we assume that

[7] *Ibid.*, pp. 94-95.

understanding will be a by-product of our instruction. We try to make ourselves knowledgeable about those subsidiary learnings that are most conducive to the promotion of understanding and then proceed to teach and test for them....

* * *

The promotion of moral conduct is analogous in some respects to the promotion of understanding. We cannot teach understanding. Nor can we "teach" moral conduct if we construe it in sense (d) above. What we can do is to promote moral conduct by providing the means by which students can arrive at beliefs, defend them, demonstrate a commitment to them, and develop a method for criticizing them.

* * *

If we seriously set about to promote understanding in the pupil we are reasonably specific about the types of understanding we wish to promote. We then choose a set of rules, techniques, and principles which will be most conducive to the promotion of that understanding, and teach directly for them. For the teacher this necessitates a ruthless process of choosing and specifying objectives of instruction, and then formulating means by which these objectives can be most efficiently attained. When testing for the attainment of them, our tests must be specific and must deal with the subject matter chosen for instruction. If our teaching has been successful, learning will have taken place. The knowledge derived will pertain not only to the specific subject matter used as a means of attaining knowledge, but to analogous situations as well. We assume that there will be a transfer of learning to other situations. If such transfer were not possible we would need to start afresh every time we taught anything.[8]

In promoting moral conduct our task is similar. We aim at the acquisition of certain principles, skills and dispositions, but we are definitely limited, for example, in the number of rules and principles that can be taught, and in the scope of skills we can teach for specifically and directly. Here again we must assume a transfer in knowledge of principles, and skills, to wider areas of experience analogous to those taught for specifically in the teaching interval.

In promoting moral conduct, then, we are concerned with achiev-

[8]In this regard see Israel Scheffler, "Justifying Curriculum Decisions," *The School Review*, Winter, 1958, pp. 470-472.

ing objectives conducive to its attainment. Chiefly, these objectives are a knowledge of moral principles, a commitment to certain of them, and the ability and tendency reflectively to support moral convictions objectively arrived at. We have suggested that the true indicator of the objectives of moral instruction is the test that is given to determine its success or failure. How then, would we test for the achievement of these objectives? We could do so by getting our students to present defensible moral positions and to indicate their convictions on ethical issues. We could teach for these objectives by presenting problems for apprehension and solution.[9] Are we then, not open to the charge that the attainment of these objectives, as measured by the tests we have designed, yields evidence only of intellectual apprehension of norms, and that we have not really striven for the attainment of those objectives that will promote moral conduct? We are presenting problems for intellectual apprehension and solution, but the *manner* in which these problems are studied and solved, and the manner in which norms are criticized represents moral activity of a significant kind. If the student is involved in an active formulation, critique, and defense of norms he is engaged in moral activity. Moral instruction thus construed aims at (a) intellectual commitment to norms; (b) reflection and criticism of norms held; (c) inculcation and promotion of a method of objective criticism and evaluation which in itself represents an important form of moral activity. Developing skill in scientific method involves the use of rules of evidence and procedure. Historical analysis involves considerable honesty in scholarship. The teacher of literature deals constantly with the understanding and resolution of moral problems.

These points suggest two implications. The first is that the process of reflecting on and criticizing norms is in itself moral activity, even though it takes place intellectually. The second is that in moral instruction, as in all other instruction, we assume that there will be a great deal of transfer (intellectual, to be sure) from the limited area of instruction to a wider range of situations in present and later life. In these important aspects moral instruction is analogous to instruction in other areas.

At this point we can postulate a notion of responsibility for the school in moral instruction. It should not aim directly for the attain-

[9]These problems, of course, need not be those of "pure" ethical character generally associated with courses in moral philosophy. They might well be issues that arise in the normal course of study that have ethical implications.

ment of moral conduct except insofar as the conduct can be taught for in the intellectual curriculum. (It is also necessary, of course, to *train* the child in practical moral matters). But that curriculum is pregnant with possibilities for moral instruction. Indeed, it might be argued that the successful teaching of history, literature and science necessitates the reflection on, discussion of and criticism of moral issues in an objective and impartial fashion.[10]

Thus we see that successful intellectual instruction often involves moral instruction, and that the successful attainment of the objectives of intellectual instruction entails the attainment of skills, attitudes and commitments that are essential to the acquisition of moral conduct. Specifically, this entails getting the student to arrive at a position on issues that are moral, justifying that position, and demonstrating consistency in its application to other moral issues.

This indicates the manner in which moral instruction can take place, as well as the limits of the school's responsibility for it. The school should not directly strive to achieve aims that promote moral conduct except insofar as this is possible and feasible within the bounds of normal intellectual curriculum study. But as we have seen this gives a considerable responsibility to the school for developing habits, skills and sensitivities that are conducive to moral conduct.[11] If the student later fails to exercise these capacities in which success has been demonstrated, we must then attribute this to a failure of the will rather than a failure of instruction.

Perhaps the principal point to be made here is that the dichotomy

[10]Of course, this is not meant to suggest that the direct inculcation of norms should not take place at appropriate points. It is an essential function of schooling. Yet it in itself, as Scheffler so clearly demonstrates, is not moral conduct. However, we should also note, that in using examples of practical maxims such as "honesty is the best policy" and "pay your debts" Scheffler unwittingly focuses too often on the area of practical maxims that are conducive to inculcation by training.

[11]Bertrand Russell shares this point of view. Taking his cue from Aristotle's analysis of the relation between intellectual and moral virtues, he says:

Although improvement of character should not be the aim of instruction, there are certain qualities which are very desirable, and which are essential to the successful pursuit of knowledge; they may be called the intellectual virtues. These should result from intellectual education; but they should result as needed in learning, not as virtues pursued for their own sakes. Among such qualities the chief seem to me: curiosity, open-mindedness, belief that knowledge is possible though difficult, patience, industry, concentration and exactness.

suggested by the distinction between "intellectual" and "moral" instruction is not necessarily valid. As several recent writers have pointed out, the *manner* in which the process of instruction is carried out is a crucial factor in developing moral sensitivity, even in the supposedly "morally neutral" field of science. Demonstrated success in the techniques and procedures of valid investigation and conclusion in these disciplines does represent a form of *moral* activity, behavior which will hopefully transfer to wider areas of moral experience. It is, in an important sense, a training of the *will*.

Now if we return to the distinction posed by Scheffler between an active and non-active interpretation of norm-stating sentences, we see that a strict interpretation of his distinction would insist on a decision between the two. What I am essentially suggesting here is that the (active)-(non-active) distinction, although valid, implies a decision between mere verbalism and real moral conduct. Although a reasonable choice suggests that the desirable alternative is the inactive one, we need not acccept the notion that this choice implies condoning a kind of vacuous verbalism. For an "inactive" interpretation, when construed in the fashion that I have described above, can be reasonably considered to be quite "active" indeed. It provides for rigorous intellectial activity that is conducive to moral conduct, but does not insure moral conduct. The choice of this construction would allow for the retention of the academic curriculum with its disciplined modes of thinking that are generalizable to a wide variety of situations. It would help to break down the dichotomy between intellectual and moral education and that between education and training. And it would remove the temptation to make the school a laboratory for experimenting with realistic, life-like situations in order to insure moral conduct on the part of its products. . . .

*   *   *

Summary

To summarize, I have suggested that Israel Scheffler's analysis of certain problems in moral education has been most helpful in clarifying the concept and in posing alternatives for decision. Since his purpose was to clarify and not to direct judgment, he is not responsible for inferences that might be drawn from his analysis. However, his distinction between an active and non-active interpretation of norm-stating sentences tends to create the impression that the normal liberal curriculum, which emphasizes an intellectual apprehension of norms, is impotent in promoting moral conduct because it rests on verbalism. This distinction tends, in its present form, to obscure the responsibility of the school and the teacher regarding moral instruction. One could easily infer that the school must teach directly for moral conduct in practical, life-like situations.

This is difficult, if not impossible, and it is undesirable, for it would, in effect, convert the school into a moral training ground at the expense of its other functions.

I suggest, then that we invoke two other notions of Mr. Scheffler's to help clarify the school's responsibility: (a) Generalizability or logical transfer[12] and (b) the importance of manner,[13] a concept which is stressed rather brilliantly by R. S. Peters.[14] When these two notions are applied to the intellectual apprehension and judgment of norms we see this "mere intellectual process" as a highly active one which is applicable in principle to a wide variety of moral situations. We also see that the student has been trained in the art of judgment and evaluation. Success in this endeavor does not insure moral conduct. Further, it does not even have as an aim of instruction moral action in life-like situations. This is a hoped for by-product of the acquisition of the aims (i.e., it is an *end* of education).

However, it would be dangerous to believe that success in moral instruction in this sense would be trivial or vacuous. For although it is true that knowing the good does not guarantee the doing of it, it is similarly true that an absence of knowledge of the good and skill in judging the good often makes moral conduct impossible, even if one desires to do the good and has the will to do so....

* * *

Perhaps, then, we have ample opportunity, within the liberal arts and sciences, to engage in moral instruction which will be conducive to moral conduct, but which will not insure it.

[12]Scheffler, "Justifying Curriculum Decisions," *op. cit.*, p. 470.
[13]Scheffler, *The Language of Education, op. cit.*, p. 58.
[14]*Authority, Responsibility and Education.* London, George Allen and Unwin Ltd., 1959, "Must an Educator have an Aim?", pp. 83-96.

XV

*Teaching for Value Clarity**

LOUIS RATHS, MERRILL HARMIN, SIDNEY SIMON

Earlier we noted some of the uncertain and confusing aspects of society and speculated upon the difficulties children have in making sense of it all. We also said that we use the term "value" to denote those beliefs, purposes, attitudes, and so on that are chosen freely and thoughtfully, prized, and acted upon. We suggested, further, that since the development of society and the people in it is best seen as dynamic, it is perhaps wiser to focus upon the process of *valuing* than upon any particular values themselves.

Now let us be a bit more explicit about that process. What, according to the theory that we propose, does one *do* if one wants to take on the problem of helping children develop values? Briefly, one assists children in using the process of valuing. The process flows naturally from the definition of values presented earlier. That is, an adult who would help children develop values would be advised to:

1. Encourage children to make choices, and to make them freely.
2. Help them discover and examine available alternatives when faced with choices.
3. Help children weigh alternatives thoughtfully, reflecting on the consequences of each.

*Reprinted with permission of the publisher from *Values and Teaching,* by Raths, Harmin, and Simon (Columbus, Ohio: Charles E. Merrill Books, 1966), pp. 38-48 and 259-261.

4. Encourage children to consider what it is that they prize and cherish.

5. Give them opportunities to make public affirmations of their choices.

6. Encourage them to act, behave, live in accordance with their choices.

7. Help them to examine repeated behaviors or patterns in their life.

In this way, the adult encourages the process of valuing. The intent of this process is to help children (although it is equally applicable to adults) clarify for themselves what they value. This is very different from trying to persuade children to accept some predetermined set of values. It is based on a conception of democracy that says persons can learn to make their own decisions. It is also based on a conception of humanity that says human beings hold the possibility of being thoughtful and wise and that the most appropriate values will come when persons use their intelligence freely and reflectively to define their relationships with each other and with an ever-changing world. Furthermore, it is based on the idea that values are personal things if they exist at all, that they cannot be personal until they are freely accepted, and that they cannot be of much significance if they do not penetrate the living of the person who holds them.

The next section of this book [Part Three] describes the value clarifying process in much more detail and gives many examples of how it might be used by teachers at many grade levels and in many subject areas. At this point it might be useful to contrast the value clarifying approach with more traditional approaches to values.

Traditional Approaches to Values

Here are some ways that have often been advocated for helping children develop values.

1. *Setting an example* either directly, by the way adults behave, or indirectly, by pointing to good models in the past or present, such as Washington's honesty or the patience of Ulysses' wife.

2. *Persuading and convincing* by presenting arguments and reasons for this or that set of values and by pointing to the fallacies and pitfalls of other sets of values.

3. *Limiting choices* by giving children choices only among values

"we" accept, such as asking children to choose between helping wash the dishes or helping clean the floor, or by giving children choices between a value we accept and one no one is likely to accept, such as asking children to choose between telling the truth and never speaking to anyone again.

4. *Inspiring* by dramatic or emotional pleas for certain values, often accompanied by models of behavior associated with the value.

5. *Rules and regulations* intended to contain and mold behavior until it is unthinkingly accepted as "right," as through the use of rewards and punishments to reinforce certain behavior.

6. *Cultural or religious dogma* presented as unquestioned wisdom or principle, such as saying that something should be believed because "our people have always done it this way."

7. *Appeals to conscience,* appeals to the still, small voice that we assume is within the heart of everyone, with the arousing of feelings of guilt if one's conscience doesn't suggest the "right" way, such as telling a child that he should know better or that he shamed his parents.

We have no doubt that such methods as those listed, and there are others that could be listed, have in the past controlled behavior and even formed beliefs and attitudes, but we assert that they have not *and cannot* lead to values in the sense that we are concerned with them—values that represent the free and thoughtful choice of intelligent humans interacting with complex and changing environments.

In fact, those methods do not seem to have resulted in deep commitments of any sort. The values that are supposedly being promoted by those methods in our society—honor, courage, devotion, self-control, craftsmanship, thrift, love, etc.—seem less than ever to be the values that guide the behavior of citizens. On the pragmatic test of effectiveness alone, the approaches listed above must receive a low grade. They just do not seem to work very well. This alone would suggest that we try a new approach.

We emphasize that these methods are not without some useful effect. It is certainly useful, for example, for adults to set examples for the kinds of behaviors that they say they support. Also, most of us have had our lives stirred and enriched by inspiring words and deeds. And many have found that religion is able to nourish virtue and hope, even in an otherwise desperate and dark life. Our main point, then, is not that the above approaches to values have been without use, but that they have not worked as well as we might have hoped and that we now have some understanding of why this might have been.

The reader will note that with each of the above approaches there is the idea of persuasion. The "right" values are predetermined and it is one method or another of selling, pushing, urging those values upon others. All the methods have the air of indoctrination, with some merely more subtle than others. The idea of free inquiry, thoughtfulness, reason seems to be lost. The approach seems not to be how to help the child develop a valuing process but, rather, how to persuade the child to adopt the "right" values.

When we ask persons why such persuasive approaches are employed, why there is little effort to have the child think through issues and freely choose what *he* prizes, we tend to receive certain answers.

1. "Children are not old enough or experienced enough or wise enough to choose values for themselves. We are responsible for starting them off on the right track. We have to drill values into children now; later they will learn to value for themselves."

The assumption here is that one does not have to practice valuing for oneself at an early age and that after twenty years or so of indoctrination one can readily break the habit of conforming to the values of others.

2. "It takes too much time to help children figure out their own values. It's faster and simpler to merely show them the best way."

There are probably assumptions here about what is most important for a limited amount of time and energy, with an implication that something other than values is most important. Also implied is the assumption that everyone can get values from being shown "the best way," even as we note that a child is exposed to many varied models of what are touted as "best ways." Note also the implication that the best ways are already defined in such a form as to be generally applicable.

3. "You can't really trust children to choose the values that would serve them best. Both their inexperience and some tendency to obstinacy may lead them to poor choices. We may have disastrous results, and most certainly we will have many regrettable results."

This view assumes that one would have children choose in all areas, whether they understood the alternatives or not and whether the choice could lead to disaster or not. It also reflects some limited faith in the intelligence and good will of children.

4. "Think of the problems that will develop from wrong choices! Time wasted, unnecessary hurt and pain, and perhaps even irreparable human damage. Besides, how can adults contain themselves when they see children going astray? What, after all, are adults for if they do not point the way to wisdom and righteousness?"

There are two separate sets of assumptions here. One set has to do with the problem of "poor" choices, which assumes that children cannot learn from such choices, that the consequences of such choices are not educational, and, in fact, that children can learn about values *without* making some poor choices. There is the idea that one is helping if he prevents a child from making a mistake.

The second set of assumptions, more by implication, seems to say that adults will feel some loss of function, perhaps of power, if they do not intervene in the decisions of children. One almost imagines an adult looking back at a long childhood of being manipulated at the whimsy of the surrounding adults and hoping that his turn to assert himself will not be denied.

5. "Look, what can I do? Everyone else tries to give values to children. My children will think I'm crazy if I do otherwise, and certainly other adults will look at me and wonder at my laxness."

This says quite plainly that many adults feel pressure from others to conform in some way. It would be unwise to underestimate the strength behind that pressure, but it tends to assume that adults under pressure have not the wherewithal to assert whatever values they hold. For some, this may be true. But it may be a result of an adult's own lack of values. One might assume that if a person didn't have a clear set of values in a certain area, he would be likely to look around and see what others are doing. Thus, some conformity is not the result of a desire to conform, but represents a desire to do what is best in circumstances which are unclear. Perhaps, then, clarity here as elsewhere is what is needed.

6. "I really do not want to get too deeply into examinations of values. It is too confusing and I do not understand it well enough myself. Maybe professionals can do it, but it is much easier to let things be and direct my attention to other things."

The assumption that is clearest here is that an adult should not work with children in areas in which he is not expert, that it would be too threatening to do so. There may also be an implication that some adults do not want to recognize how ineffective their own valuing process has been.

7. "It is a matter of will power. If one wants to do something, all he needs is the will to do it."

This assumes, of course, that one does want to do something, that purposes are clear, that something is blocking the achievement of personal goals. It does not seem to take in the possibility that purposes are not clear and that ambivalence is in control.

8. "Frankly, children are more difficult to handle if they are deciding too many things for themselves. If children expect to learn what they should believe and value from us, it is easier all around. There will be fewer discipline problems."

The assumption here is that children who are tractable are more valuable than children who have values. There is the additional assumption that the indoctrination of values does lead to more obedient children and fewer behavior problems.

9. "Children appreciate being told what to do and what to believe. It gives them security. Freedom is frightening to many of them."

The assumption here would seem to deal with the cause of insecurity that arises when duties cease to direct children. Are children insecure only because they now would have free time and free choice, or are they insecure because they have had no help in acquiring real values to direct their use of that freedom? Is the answer to keep children under pressure, keep them busy, keep them under control? Or is the answer to help them to develop values so that they can be responsibly self-directing in an ever-changing world?

Now these reasons for wanting to persuade children to take on certain values seem to us to be based on questionable assumptions, although some of the assumptions seem more temptingly tenable than others and some are probably reasonable for some situations and not for others. There is at least one additional reason for adults trying to impose their values on children, and it is perhaps the overriding reason:

no other alternative that is clear and testable has been provided. Not being aware of another choice, who can blame adults for doing what they think best? The observation that many children and adults do not, in fact, seem to have many clear values may have raised questions about the efficiency of trying to sell adult beliefs to children, but what alternative choice is there? This book, of course, hopes to offer one.

Why a New Approach?

There is widespread concern that youth, and adults in some cases, do not seem to live by any consistent set of values. They act impetuously, erratically, and sometimes with malice. Many children find nothing enjoyable to do with their free time. Even in school many seem purposeless and listless, motivated only—but not always consistently—by outside pressures. Our population is becoming other-directed, it is asserted; we guide our lives not by what we believe is right and proper, but by what others do or say. Does this not suggest that many persons have unclear values?

We note the wide discrepancy between what people do and what they say. Many political leaders, business executives, military leaders, workers of all sorts, and even professional people are known to *do* things that are inconsistent with what they *say* are their values. Corruption is not an unusual occurrence. So many people can be "bought." Does this not suggest that the approaches to values that have been so widely used in the past have been less than effective?

Adults have been trying to set examples for years. They have tried often with ingenious manipulation to persuade children to accept certain values. They have carefully limited choices given to children. They have attempted to inspire identification with particular values. They have made rules and insisted on certain patterns of behavior. They have relied upon religion and cultural truisms. They have appealed to the consciences of young people. But even a casual look at the results of these approaches is discouraging. They just do not seem to have worked.

In the past we have told children, children who have been exposed to so many different and confusing stimuli, that they should believe in one thing or another. We have said this in many ways: by our example, our rules, our arguments, and so on. But as we spoke, they were surrounded by other examples and arguments which stood for different values; and when a child indicated by a lack of purpose or a disregard of purpose that he was confused by all this, we insisted, punished, pleaded, and otherwise campaigned even harder for one of the many values that we were convinced he must adopt. More than likely this only further confused many children and made them less able to decide in what to believe. Consequently, many children pretend to believe. Or if they do believe, they try not to do it very keenly. Or they deal with the dilemma by taking whatever belief is popular and convenient at the moment, switching frequently.

Why must teachers see their role only as putting things into the mind of the child? Why can't a role be defined that would help a child take all the confusion that already exists in his mind, remove it, look at it, examine it, turn it around, and make some order out of it? Why can't teachers learn to spend some of their time helping children understand what the bewildering array of beliefs and attitudes that saturate our modern life are all about and which suits him best? Is this not the road to values, to *clear* and *personal* values?

We believe it is. We believe that as children are helped to use what we call the valuing process, they will move toward value clarity in a more sensible and dramatic way than ever before. Peck and Havighurst put it succinctly:

> It is temptingly easy and insidiously gratifying to "mold" children, or to "whip them into line" by exercising one's superior status and authority as an adult. It is often personally inconvenient to allow children time to debate alternatives, and it may be personally frustrating if their choice contradicts one's own preferences. If there is any selfish, sensitive "pride" at stake, it is very hard for most adults to refrain from controlling children in an autocratic manner. Then, too, like any dictatorship, it looks "more efficient"—to the dictator, at least. However, the effect on character is to arrest the development of rational judgment and to create such resentments as prevent the growth of genuine altruistic impulses. For thousands of years, the long-term effects have been ignored and sacrificed to short-term adult advantages, most of the time. Probably it is no accident that there are relatively few people who are, or ever will become, psychologically and ethically mature.[1]

[1] R. Peck and R. Havighurst, *The Psychology of Character Development* (New York: John Wiley and Sons, 1960), p. 191.

Summary of Part Two

So far we have presented a view of the concept of value that is based on a particular notion of human potential, one which emphasizes man's capacity for intelligent, self-directed behavior. We have said that it would be well to reserve the term "value" for those individual beliefs, attitudes, activities, or feelings that satisfy the criteria of (1) having been freely chosen, (2) having been chosen from among alternatives, (3) having been chosen after due reflection, (4) having been prized and cherished, (5) having been publicly affirmed, (6) having been incorporated into actual behavior, and (7) having been repeated in one's life. In different words, we might say that something will not qualify as a value if *any* of the following conditions apply.

1. It has not been *freely* chosen (no room in this theory for values that are imposed upon one by outside pressures).

2. It is without one or more available alternatives (a real choice must exist, not a spurious choice).

3. It has been chosen without thoughtful consideration (this excludes impulse or highly emotional choices from the category of values).

4. It is not prized or cherished (we exclude from the level of values those things which we have or do of which we are not proud and would rather not have or do—as when one chooses the least objectionable of several undesirable alternatives).

5. It is denied upon public confrontation (to be ashamed or unduly fearful of something is to indicate that one does not value it highly).

6. It is not in some way reflected in one's actual behavior (one who chooses democracy and never does anything to put that choice into practice may be said to have an attitude or belief about democracy but not a value).

7. It is a passing fancy and lacks any persistence over time (a one-shot effort at pottery-making, for example, would not qualify as a value).

The meaning here for schools and, more particularly, the busy classroom teacher is implicit in the definition. If one wishes to help children develop clearer values, one must help children use the process of valuing. That is, one must help children: (1) make free choices whenever possible, (2) search for alternatives in choice-making situations, (3) weigh the consequences of each available alternative, (4) consider what they prize and cherish, (5) affirm the things they value,

(6) do something about their choices, and (7) consider and strengthen patterns in their lives. It is as simple, and complex, as that. As the teacher helps students use these processes, he helps them find values.

It should be increasingly clear that the adult does not force his own pet values upon children. What he does is create conditions that aid children in finding values *if* they choose to do so. When operating with this value theory, it is entirely possible that children will choose not to develop values. It is the teacher's responsibility to support this choice also, while at the same time realizing that value development is likely to be one of the goals of the school and, if so, it should be encouraged by providing regular experiences that will help raise to the value level the beliefs, feelings, interests, and activities children bring with them.

The teacher who activates the value theory . . . can expect that children will have more values, be more aware of the values that they have, have values that are more consistent with one another, and especially, be ready to use the valuing process as they continue to grow and learn.

But there are also purposes that are more concrete, more relevant to the typical school task, and more readily measurable that seem to be promoted by the valuing process. For example, research . . . shows that when the valuing process was promoted with children who were very apathetic, over-conforming, flighty, and likely to act in a variety of poses or "phony" roles, this type of behavior became noticeably less acute and less frequent. There is also evidence that these techniques help children who are very indecisive, who are very inconsistent, or who are chronic dissenters. Other research showed the valuing process to help underachievers improve in the following:

> Attitudes toward learning
> Raising of questions and alternatives
> Initiation and self-direction of classroom activity
> Perseverance
> Active participation

In general, the research shows that students become more vital and purposeful when given opportunities to clarify their values. . . .

*   *   *

[Following is the authors' outline of topics covered in their chapters on specific teaching procedures.]

Notes

THE SEVEN VALUING CRITERIA
1. Choosing from alternatives
2. Choosing after careful consideration of the consequences of each alternative
3. Choosing freely
4. Prizing, being glad of one's choice
5. Prizing, being willing to publicly affirm one's choice
6. Acting upon one's choice, incorporating choices into behavior
7. Acting upon one's choice repeatedly, over time

VALUE INDICATORS
1. Goals or purposes
2. Aspirations
3. Attitudes
4. Interests
5. Feelings
6. Beliefs and convictions
7. Activities
8. Worries, problems, obstacles

VALUE-RELATED BEHAVIORAL PROBLEM TYPES
1. The apathetic, listless, disinterested person
2. The flighty person
3. The very uncertain
4. The very inconsistent
5. The drifting person
6. The overconforming person
7. The overdissenting person
8. The role-playing person

TEN VALUE-RICH AREAS
1. Money
2. Friendship
3. Love and sex
4. Religion and morals
5. Leisure
6. Politics and social organization

7. Work
8. Family
9. Maturity
10. Character traits

THIRTY CLARIFYING RESPONSES

1. Is this something that you prize?
2. Are you glad about that?
3. How did you feel when that happened?
4. Did you consider any alternatives?
5. Have you felt this way for a long time?
6. Was that something that you yourself selected or chose?
7. Did you *have* to choose that; was it a free choice?
8. Do you *do* anything about that idea?
9. Can you give me some examples of that idea?
10. What do you mean by _____: can you define that word?
11. Where would that idea lead; what would be its consequences?
12. Would you really *do* that or are you just talking?
13. Are you saying that... [repeat the statement]?
14. Did you say that... [repeat in some distorted way]?
15. Have you thought much about that idea (or behavior)?
16. What are some good things about that notion?
17. What do we have to assume for things to work out that way?
18. Is what you express consistent with . . . [Note something else the person said or did that may point to an inconsistency]?
19. What other possibilities are there?
20. Is that a personal preference or do you think most people should believe that?
21. How can I help you do something about your idea?
22. Is there a purpose back of this activity?
23. Is that very important to you?
24. Do you do this often?
25. Would you like to tell others about your idea?
26. Do you have any reasons for saying (or doing) that?
27. Would you do the same thing over again?
28. How do you know it's right?
29. Do you value that?
30. Do you think people will always believe that?

TWENTY-ONE CLARIFYING STRATEGIES

1. The clarifying response
2. The value sheet
3. The value-clarifying discussion
4. Role-playing
5. The contrived incident
6. Zig-zag lessons
7. Devil's advocate
8. Value continuum
9. Thought sheets
10. Weekly reaction sheets
11. Open-ended questions
12. Coded student papers
13. Time diaries
14. Autobiographical questionnaires
15. Public interviews
16. Decision-making interviews
17. Voting
18. Five-minute quotes without comment
19. Student reports
20. Action projects
21. An approach to self-conception

A Final Word

Three main challenges face those concerned with contemporary moral education. The first of these is to make more apparent the nature and complexity of the moral sphere and of moral education as implied by the tradition of moral philosophy. To help meet this challenge has been our chief endeavor in this volume.

The second and third challenges will ultimately be more decisive.

The second frontier of moral education is the accumulation of indispensable empirical knowledge about the nature of moral development in the young. Notions of the child as a moral midget who will sprout more or less suddenly into a moral adult are at best insufficiently verified and at worst constitute a distorted caricature. (Psychological research conclusions conforming to such representations may, as Kohlberg indicates, reflect philosophical and educational assumptions of the researcher.) What is needed now is serious and concentrated empirical study of the nature of moral life and development, based on sounder philosophical assumptions than those of traditional psychology and sociology. (Both Piaget's and Kohlberg's work may be seen as valuable movement in this direction.)

The third challenge to moral education is the development of curricula and teaching materials which reflect a sophisticated and complicated conception of moral education. There are two valuable resources for the development of such moral education programs: moral philosophy, as a source of clarification and exposition of key concepts, contents, and directions for moral education; and new curricula in traditional subject matter areas, as models of a procedure for development of sophisticated educational materials. Moral philosophy is able to indicate what components are essential for moral education programs; the methodology of the new curricula can point to ways in which such programs might be developed.

The problems of teaching moral values must not be minimized; neither, however, can they excuse neglect. The resources for serious work in moral education far outstrip the observable efforts or outcomes in contemporary attempts at educating the young for the moral life. As we have attempted to show in this volume, there is a plentiful traditional literature of moral philosophy which can elucidate the most "practical" problems of the educational sphere. Moreover, the mass media, school life, and the child's own experiences give moral issues an immediacy hardly to be matched in any mere "subject" area of the school curriculum. And finally, there do exist certain educational patterns and guidelines for the translation of sophisticated contents into understandable and teachable materials. The paucity of effort in moral education, then, is perhaps reflective of the most distressing of all educational inadequacies—the kind that are rooted in the failure of human volition, and in ignorance.

Bibliographic Note

The literature on and related to moral education is plentiful, consequently demanding appropriate categorization and selection. In this Note we refer to sources by numbers locating them in the categories of the Bibliography itself.

Literature in moral philosophy obviously constitutes a central resource for the study of moral education. Whether one effects this correlation between moral philosophy and moral education by initially focusing on major classics in ethics (a concise list of which appears in Broudy, Parsons, Snook, and Szoke, 1.2) and moving from there to relevant problems of education, or, as R. S. Peters suggests (and as exemplified in his *Ethics and Education* 1.13), by focusing on central problems of moral education and then tracing their philosophic roots, will depend largely on individual proclivities and professional contingencies. The important point is that any discussion of moral education must include a clear analysis of the basic concepts, problems, and discussions of moral philosophy.

There are several introductory volumes which are of value in this context, e.g., Frankena 1.6, Hospers 1.8, Montefiore 1.11, and Nowell-Smith 1.13. The Wallace-Walker anthology, although not an introductory volume, is an excellent collection of recent philosophical essays dealing with the definition of "morality." It is important to note that introductory volumes sometimes represent and argue for a particular moral philosophical position, and in such cases they are more valuable as expositions of alternative philosophic schools than as general introductions to the field (Hare 1.8 and Nowell-Smith 1.13 are examples of this).

Beyond the introductory volumes, reference should be made to the extensive and detailed analyses of specific issues in moral philosophy, as illustrated in categories 2, 3, 4, 5. Such a literature focuses in great detail on selected problems and issues of moral philosophy, rather than attempting to map out the field in its entirety. In addition, the literature of moral philosophy reflects much dialogue and interchange between philosophers vis-à-vis the analysis of specific issues. In the case of traditional moral philosophy, this usually manifests itself in close studies and critiques of classical works. In the case of contemporary moral philosophy this phenomenon usually manifests itself in the back-and-forth discussion between authors of books and articles and their critics. It is an extremely valuable learning device to trace this kind of reciprocal discussion in such journals as *Mind, Proceedings of the Aristotelian Society, Ethics, Journal of Philosophy, Studies in Philosophy and Education, Philosophical Review, Philosophy, and Philosophical Quarterly.*

In the educational sphere there are at least three categories of literature on moral education. The first deals with the nature of existing programs of moral education and/or offers programmatic suggestions for improvement. Such a literature is frequently practical and immediate in nature, and may be found in publications of central departments of education, teachers' pamphlets, principals' memos, and popular education journals.

A second category of literature is in the sphere of philosophy of education and analysis of educational concepts. Most introductory texts and lectures on philosophy of education deal with "moral education" as a central issue (the Broudy, Parsons, Snook, Szoke volume 1.2 contains a comprehensive listing of sources up to 1966). In addition the major education journals, e.g., *Teachers College Record, Harvard Educational Review, School Review, Educational Theory, Educational Philosophy and Theory,* frequently include discussions of important issues of moral education. The journal *Moral Education,* published in England by the Farmington Research Trust, deals with such issues exclusively.

A third category of sources relevant to moral education is the literature of the social sciences which deals with moral development and the moral life. A good introduction to this sphere may be found in the Williams and Sugarman sections of the Wilson volume 4.10, in Kay's *Moral Development* 4.2, in Kohlberg's new volume 4.3, and in Dreeben 5.2. The studies of Hartshorne and May 5.4, Piaget 5.10, Peck and Havighurst 5.9, and Durkheim 6.5, are basic. In the case of such literature it is important to remember the qualification previously noted, namely that such studies operate on the basis of and reflect a certain conception of morality, rather than explaining and explicating alternative notions. Thus, it is important at the outset to have a clear picture of the conception of morality implicit in respective empirical studies.

A final category of sources on moral education (which has not been included in this bibliography) is the literature of moralizing and moral criticism. There are some very good and very bad examples of moral fervor, passion, and exhortation in contemporary essays, fiction, drama, sermons, speeches, and educational critiques. This literature is valuable when viewed in the proper perspective.

In general the key to maximizing the utility of the resource literature of moral education is a clear conception of the nature of the questions being asked or the problems being faced, and of the sources most appropriate to the answering of specific questions and problems. Such a clarity of conception vis-à-vis the problems being faced is an essential precondition for any sort of meaningful confrontation with the variegated literature of moral education and it has been one of the purposes of this volume to provide such a perspective for the reader.

Bibliography

1. Morality and Moral Philosophy

1. Aiken, Henry D. "Moral Philosophy and Education," *Harvard Educational Review* XXV (Winter, 1955).
2. Broudy, Harry S.; Parsons, Michael J.; Snook, Ivan A.; & Szoke, Ronald S. *Philosophy of Education.* Urbana: University of Illinois Press, 1967.
3. Dewey, John. *Theory of the Moral Life.* New York: Holt, Rinehart and Winston, 1908.
4. Feinberg, Joel, editor. *Moral Concepts.* London: Oxford University Press, 1967.
5. Foot, Phillipa. *Theories of Ethics.* London: Oxford University Press, 1967.
6. Frankena, William. *Ethics.* Englewood Cliffs, N.J.: Prentice-Hall, Inc., 1963.
7. _____. "Recent Conceptions of Morality," in *Morality: The Language of Conduct,* Hector-Neri Castaneda and George Naknikian, editors. Detroit: Wayne State University Press, 1963.
8. Hare, R. M. *The Language of Morals.* New York: Oxford University Press, 1964.
9. _____. *Freedom and Reason.* New York: Oxford University Press, 1965.
10. Hospers, J. *Human Conduct: An Introduction to the Problems of Ethics.* New York: Harcourt, Brace and World, 1961.

11. Kerner, George. *The Revolution in Ethical Theory*. New York: Oxford University Press, 1966.
12. Montefiore, Alan. *A Modern Introduction to Moral Theory*. London: Routledge and Kegan Paul, 1958.
13. _____. "Moral Philosophy and the Teaching of Morality." *Harvard Educational Review* XXXV (Fall, 1965).
14. Nowell-Smith, P. H. *Ethics*. London: Penguin Books, 1954.
15. Peters, R. S. *Ethics and Education*. New York: Scott, Foresman and Company, 1967.
16. Wallace, G., & Walker, A. D. M., editors. *The Definition of Morality*. London: Methuen and Company, Ltd., 1970.
17. Warnock, G. J. *Contemporary Moral Philosophy*. London: Macmillan and Company, Ltd., 1967.
18. Warnock, Mary. *Ethics Since 1900*. London: Oxford University Press, 1960.

2. The Justification of Morality

1. Griffiths, A. P. "Justifying Moral Principles." *Proceedings of the Aristotelian Society*, 1957-1958.
2. Moore, G. E. *Ethics*. New York: Oxford University Press, 1965.
3. _____. *Principia Ethica*. Cambridge: Cambridge University Press, 1922.
4. Peters, R. S. "Classical Theories of Justification," in R. S. Peters, *Ethics and Education*. New York: Scott, Foresman and Company, 1967.
5. Rich, John Martin. "Teaching the Justifications for the Moral Life." *Educational Theory* LXV (October, 1964).
6. Warnock, G. J. *Contemporary Moral Philosophy*. London: Macmillan and Company, Ltd., 1967.

3. Moral Principles

1. Baier, K. *The Moral Point of View*. Ithaca: Cornell University Press, 1958.
2. Dewey, John. *Moral Principles in Education*. New York: Houghton Mifflin Company, 1909.
3. Foot, P. R. "When Is a Principle a Moral Principle?" *Proceedings of the Aristotelian Society*, Supplementary Volume, 1954.
4. Hare, R. M. *The Language of Morals*. New York: Oxford University Press, 1964.
5. Rawls, John. "Two Concepts of Rules." *Philosophical Review* LXIV (1955), 3-32.

6. Singer, Marcus. *Generalization in Ethics.* New York: Alfred A. Knopf, 1961.
7. _____. "Moral Rules and Principles," in *Essays in Moral Philosophy,* A. I. Melden, editor. Seattle: University of Washington Press, 1958.
8. Williamson, William. "Moral-Spiritual Values." *Teachers College Record* LXVIII (April, 1967).

4. Moral Thinking and Autonomy

1. Aiken, H. D. "The Concept of Moral Objectivity," in *Morality and the Language of Conduct,* H. N. Castaneda and G. Naknikian, editors. Detroit: Wayne State University Press, 1963.
2. Beardsmore, R. W. *Moral Reasoning.* London: Routledge and Keagan Paul, 1969.
3. Kay, William. *Moral Development.* London: George Allen and Unwin, 1968.
4. Kohlberg, Lawrence. "Development of Moral Character and Ideology," in *Review of Child Development Research,* M. L. Hoffman, editor (Russell Sage, 1964).
5. Maslow, A. H. *Towards a Psychology of Being.* Princeton: D. Van Nostrand, 1962.
6. Patton, Thomas. "Reasoning in Moral Matters." *Journal of Philosophy* LIII (August, 1956).
7. Rich, John Martin. *Education and Human Values.* Reading, Mass.: Addison-Wesley, 1968.
8. Toulmin, Stephen. *An Examination of the Place of Reason in Ethics.* Cambridge: Cambridge University Press, 1950.
9. Walsh, W. H. "Moral Authority and Moral Choice." *Proceedings of the Aristotelian Society,* Vol. 65.
10. Wilson, J.; Williams, N.; & Sugarman, B. *Introduction to Moral Education.* London: Penguin Books, 1967.
11. _____. *Moral Thinking.* London: Heinemann, 1970.

5. Moral Knowledge and Action

1. Bradburn, E. "Children's Moral Knowledge." *Educational Research* IX (1967).
2. Dreeben, Robert. *On What Is Learned in School.* Reading, Mass.: Addison-Wesley, 1968.
3. Frankena, William. "Toward a Philosophy of Moral Education." *Harvard Educational Review* XXVIII (Fall, 1958).
4. Hartshorne, H.; May, M.; & Shuttlesworth, F. *Studies in the Or-*

ganization of Character. New York: The Macmillan Company, 1930.

5. Kohlberg, Lawrence. *Stages in the Development of Moral Thought and Action.* New York: Holt, Rinehart and Winston, 1970.

6. Lukes, S. "Moral Weakness." *Philosophical Quarterly,* 1965.

7. Matthews, G. M. "Weakness of Will." *Mind,* 1966.

8. McGuire, M. C. "Can I Do What I Think I Ought Not To? Where Has Hare Gone Wrong?" *Mind,* 1961.

9. Peck, Robert, & Havighurst, Robert. *The Psychology of Character Development.* New York: John Wiley and Sons, Inc., 1960.

10. Piaget, J. *The Moral Development of the Child.* London: Routledge and Kegan Paul, 1932.

11. Phillips, D. Z. "Does It Pay to Be Good?" *Proceedings of the Aristotelian Society,* 1964-1965.

6. *Teaching Moral Values*

1. Allinsmith, W. "Moral Standards: The Learning of Moral Standards," in *Inner Conflict and Defense,* D. R. Miller and G. G. Swainson, editors. New York: Holt, Rinehart, and Winston, 1960.

2. Atkinson, R. F. "Instruction and Indoctrination," in *Philosophical Analysis and Education.* London: Routledge and Kegan Paul, 1965.

3. Bower, William Clayton. *Moral and Spiritual Values in Education.* Lexington: University of Kentucky Press, 1952.

4. Carbone, Peter. "Reflections on Moral Education." *Teachers College Record* LXXI (May, 1970).

5. Dewey, John. "Teaching Ethics in High School." *Educational Theory* XVII (July, 1967).

6. Fenton, Edwin. *The New Social Studies.* New York: Holt, Rinehart and Winston, Inc., 1967.

7. Flew, A. "What is Indoctrination?" *Studies in Philosophy and Education* IV (Spring, 1966).

8. Gregory, I. M., & Woods, R. G. "Indoctrination." *Proceedings of the Annual Conference,* Philosophy of Education Society of Great Britain, IV (1970).

9. Hare, R. M. "Adolescents Into Adults," in *Aims in Education: The Philosophic Approach,* T. H. B. Hollins, editor. Manchester: Manchester University Press. 1964.

10. Low-Beer, A. "Moral Judgements in History and History Teach-

ing," in *The Nature of History and History Teaching,* W. H. Burston and D. Thompson, editors. London: Routledge and Kegan Paul, 1967.

11. Massialas, Byron, & Zevin, Jack. *Creative Encounters in the Classroom.* New York: John Wiley and Sons, 1967.

12. Moore, Willis. "Indoctrination as a Normative Conception." *Studies in Philosophy and Education* IV (Summer, 1966).

13. *Moral and Spiritual Values in the Public Schools.* Washington: Educational Policies Commission, National Education Association, 1951.

14. Parsons, Talcott. "The School Class as a Social System: Some of Its Functions in American Society." *Harvard Educational Review* XXIX (Fall, 1959).

15. Peters, R. S. "Reason and Habit: The Paradox of Moral Education," in *Moral Education in a Changing Society,* W. R. Niblett, editor. London: Faber and Faber, 1963.

16. Raths, Louis; Harmin, Merrill; & Simon, Sidney. *Values and Teaching.* Columbus, Ohio: Charles E. Merrill Books, Inc., 1966.

17. Ward, Lionel. *Teaching Moral Values.* Oxford: The Religious Education Press, 1969.

18. White, J. P. "Indoctrination," in *The Concept of Education.* New York: Humanities Press, 1969.

19. _____. "Indoctrination." *Proceedings of the Annual Conference,* Philosophy of Education Society of Great Britain, IV (1970).

20. Wilson, J. *Moral Education and the Curriculum.* New York: Pergamon Press, 1969.